FAVORITE BRAND NAME™
GRILLING

Publications International, Ltd.

Favorite Brand Name Recipes at www.fbnr.com

Microwave Cooking: Microwave ovens vary in wattage. Use the cooking times as guidelines and check for doneness before adding more time.

Contents

The Heat Is On

Shimmering sunny skies and starry moonlit summer nights are the perfect background atmosphere to enjoy the time-honored tradition of great grilled food. Cooking over an open fire is the oldest cooking method known to man. Developed in a quest for survival, this ancient art has come a long way since then—new, innovative grilling and flavoring techniques add interest to all kinds of foods. Keep this favorite cooking method alive with hot and spicy "Smacking" Wings, mouthwatering Dijon Bacon Cheeseburgers and finger licking Baby Back Ribs—perfect to grace lantern-lit patios, picnic tables and even your dining room table.

BASIC FIRE

• Always place the grill on a solid surface, set away from shrubbery, grass and overhangs.

• NEVER use alcohol, gasoline or kerosene as a lighter fluid—all three can cause an explosion.

• To get a sluggish fire going, place two or three additional coals in a small metal can and add lighter fluid. Then, stack them on the coals in the grill and light with a match.

• Keep a water-filled spray bottle near the grill to quench flare-ups. (Do not use water to quench flare-ups on a gas grill. Close the hood and turn the heat down until the flaring subsides.)

• Remember: hot coals create a hot grill, grid, tools and food. Always wear heavy-duty fireproof mitts to protect your hands.

• The number of coals required for barbecuing depends on the size and type of grill and the amount of food to be prepared. As a general rule, it takes about 30 coals to grill one pound of meat.

• To light a charcoal fire, arrange the coals in a pyramid shape 20 to 30 minutes prior to cooking. The pyramid shape provides enough ventilation for the coals to catch. To start with lighter fluid, soak the coals with about ½ cup lighter fluid. Wait one minute to allow the fluid to soak into the coals and light with a match.

• To light a charcoal fire using a chimney starter, remove the grid from the grill and place the chimney starter in the base of the grill. Crumble a few sheets of newspaper and place them in the bottom portion of the chimney starter. Fill the top portion with coals. Light the newspaper. The coals should be ready in about 20 to 30 minutes.

BASIC TEMPERATURES

This chart gives the basic internal temperatures of meat to determine cooking doneness.

Meat	Doneness	Temperature
Poultry		180°F (170°F in the breast)
Pork		160°F
Beef*	Rare	140°F
	Medium-rare	150°F
	Medium	160°F
	Well Done	170°F
Lamb		160°F

*When cooking burgers using ground beef, be sure that the burgers' internal temperature reaches at least 160°F.

- The coals are ready when they are about 80% ash gray during daylight and glowing at night.

- To lower the cooking temperature, spread the coals farther apart or raise the grid. To raise the cooking temperature, either lower the grid or move the coals closer together and tap off the ash.

BASIC COOKING METHODS

Direct Cooking

The food is placed on the grid directly over the coals. Make sure there is enough charcoal in a single layer to extend 1 or 2 inches beyond the food on the grill. This method is for quick-cooking foods, such as steaks, chops, hamburgers, kabobs and fish.

Indirect Cooking

The food is placed on the grid over a metal or disposable foil drip pan with the coals banked either to one side or on both sides of the pan. This method is for slow, even cooking of foods, such as large cuts of meat and whole chickens.

When barbecuing by indirect cooking for more than 45 minutes, extra briquets will need to be added to maintain a constant temperature.

Drugstore Wrap

Place the food in the center of an oblong piece of heavy-duty foil, leaving at least a two-inch border around the food. Bring the two long sides together above the food; fold down in a series of locked folds, allowing for heat circulation and expansion.

Fold the short ends up and over again. Press folds firmly to seal the foil packet.

BASIC TIPS

- Always use tongs or a spatula when handling meat. Piercing meat with a fork allows juices to escape and makes meat less moist.

- Always serve cooked food from the grill on a clean plate, not one that held the raw food.

- Wash all utensils, cutting boards and containers with hot soapy water after they have been in contact with uncooked meat, poultry and fish.

- The cooking rack, or grid, should be kept clean and free from any bits of charred food. Scrub the grid with a stiff brush while it is still warm.

- In hot weather, food should never sit out for more than 1 hour. Remember, keep hot foods hot and cold foods cold.

- Store charcoal in a dry place. Charcoal won't burn well if it is damp.

- Top and bottom vents should be open before starting a charcoal grill. Close vents when cooking is finished to extinguish the coals.

- The best way to judge the doneness of meat is with a high-quality meat thermometer. Prior to grilling, insert the thermometer into the center of the largest muscle of the meat with the point away from bone or fat. An instant-read thermometer gives an accurate reading within seconds of insertion, although it is not heatproof and should not be left in the meat during grilling.

CHECKING CHARCOAL TEMPERATURE

A quick, easy way to estimate the temperature of the coals is to hold your hand, palm side down, about 4 inches above the coals. Count the number of seconds you can hold your hand in that position before the heat forces you to pull it away.

Seconds	Coals	Temp
2	hot	375°F or more
3	medium-hot	350° to 370°F
4	medium	300° to 350°F
5	low	200° to 300°F

Fired-Up Firsts

Honeyed Pork and Mango Kabobs (page 24)

Barbecue Beef Ribettes (page 12)

Steak Nachos

1 (1-pound) beef top round steak, chopped
¼ cup chopped onion
1 tablespoon vegetable oil
½ cup A.1.® Original or A.1.® Bold & Spicy Steak
    Sauce
5 cups tortilla chips
2 cups shredded Cheddar or Monterey Jack
    cheese (8 ounces)
1 cup chopped fresh tomatoes
¼ cup diced green chiles or jalapeño pepper
    slices
¼ cup sliced pitted ripe olives
    Dairy sour cream (optional)

In large skillet, over medium-high heat, sauté steak and onion in oil until steak is no longer pink; drain. Stir in steak sauce. Arrange tortilla chips on large heatproof platter or baking sheet. Spoon steak mixture over chips; sprinkle with cheese. Broil 6 inches from heat source 3 to 5 minutes or until cheese melts. Top with tomatoes, chiles and olives. Serve immediately with sour cream on the side, if desired.

Makes 6 appetizer servings

Chicken Kabobs with Thai Dipping Sauce

1 pound boneless skinless chicken breasts, cut into 1-inch cubes
1 small cucumber, seeded and cut into small chunks
1 cup cherry tomatoes
2 green onions, cut into 1-inch pieces
⅔ cup teriyaki baste & glaze sauce
⅓ cup FRANK'S® Original REDHOT® Cayenne Pepper Sauce
⅓ cup peanut butter
3 tablespoons frozen orange juice concentrate, undiluted
2 cloves garlic, minced

Thread chicken, cucumber, tomatoes and onions alternately onto metal skewers; set aside.

To prepare Thai Dipping Sauce, combine teriyaki baste & glaze sauce, RedHot® sauce, peanut butter, orange juice concentrate and garlic; mix well. Reserve ⅔ cup sauce for dipping.

Brush skewers with some of remaining sauce. Place skewers on oiled grid. Grill over hot coals 10 minutes or until chicken is no longer pink in center, turning and basting often with remaining sauce. Serve skewers with Thai Dipping Sauce. Garnish as desired.

Makes 6 appetizer servings

Prep Time: *15 minutes*
Cook Time: *10 minutes*

Hot Off The Grill

Always serve cooked food from the grill on a clean plate, not one that held the raw food.

Chicken Kabobs with Thai Dipping Sauce

Greek-Style Grilled Feta

¼ **cup thinly sliced sweet onion**
1 **package (8 ounces) feta cheese, sliced in half horizontally**
¼ **cup thinly sliced green bell pepper**
¼ **cup thinly sliced red bell pepper**
½ **teaspoon dried oregano leaves**
¼ **teaspoon garlic pepper or ground black pepper**
24 **(½-inch) slices French bread**

1. Spray 14-inch-long sheet of foil with nonstick cooking spray. Place onion slices in center of foil and top with feta slices. Sprinkle with bell pepper slices, oregano and garlic pepper.

2. Seal foil using Drugstore Wrap technique.* Place foil packet on grid upside down and grill on covered grill over hot coals 15 minutes. Turn packet over; grill on covered grill 15 minutes more.

3. Open packet carefully and serve immediately with slices of French bread.

Makes 8 servings

*Place the food in the center of an oblong piece of heavy-duty foil, leaving at least a two-inch border around the food. Bring the two long sides together above the food; fold down in a series of locked folds, allowing for heat circulation and expansion. Fold the short ends up and over again. Press folds firmly to seal the foil packet.

Grilled Stuffed Mushrooms

24 **large 2-inch mushrooms, wiped clean**
3 **tablespoons olive oil, divided**
1 **red bell pepper, seeded and chopped**
½ **cup minced fresh Italian parsley**
2 **tablespoons FRENCH'S® Worcestershire Sauce**
1 **teaspoon garlic powder**
1⅓ **cups FRENCH'S® French Fried Onions, divided**
½ **cup grated Parmesan cheese**

Remove stems from mushrooms. Finely chop stems; set aside. Brush mushrooms caps with 1 tablespoon oil. Place caps on a tray.

Heat remaining 2 tablespoons oil in large nonstick skillet over medium-high heat. Add chopped stems and pepper; cook and stir until tender. Stir in parsley, Worcestershire and garlic powder. Cook until liquid is evaporated, stirring often. Stir in ⅔ cup French Fried Onions and cheese.

Spoon about 1 tablespoon mushroom mixture into each mushroom cap. Place mushroom caps on vegetable grilling rack or basket. Place on grid. Grill over medium-high coals 15 minutes or until mushrooms are tender. Sprinkle with remaining ⅔ cup onions. Grill 1 minute or until onions are golden. Serve warm.

Makes 6 appetizer servings

Prep Time: *30 minutes*
Cook Time: *25 minutes*

Greek-Style Grilled Feta

Barbecue Beef Ribettes

    1 clove garlic, minced
    1 tablespoon vegetable oil
    ½ cup ketchup
    ⅓ cup A.1.® Original or A.1.®
        Bold & Spicy Steak Sauce
    ¼ cup chili sauce
    2 tablespoons firmly packed
        light brown sugar
    2 thin slices fresh lemon
    ½ teaspoon liquid hot pepper
        seasoning
    2½ pounds beef ribs, cut into
        2-inch pieces

In medium saucepan, over low heat, cook garlic in oil until tender. Stir in ketchup, steak sauce, chili sauce, sugar, lemon and hot pepper seasoning; cook 1 to 2 minutes or until heated through. Reserve ⅔ cup for serving with cooked ribs. Set aside remaining sauce for basting ribs.

Arrange ribs on rack in large roasting pan. Bake at 400°F 30 minutes.

Brush ribs generously with ¼ cup basting sauce. Grill ribs over medium heat or broil 6 inches from heat source 20 to 25 minutes or until ribs are tender, turning and basting often with remaining basting sauce. Serve with reserved ⅔ cup sauce. Garnish as desired.   *Makes 8 appetizer servings*

"Smoking" Wings

    16 chicken wings
    ½ cup olive or vegetable oil
    ¼ cup balsamic vinegar
    ¼ cup honey
    2 tablespoons brown sugar
    2 tablespoons cane syrup or
        dark corn syrup
    1 tablespoon TABASCO®
        brand Pepper Sauce
    ½ teaspoon red pepper flakes
    ½ teaspoon dried thyme leaves
    1 teaspoon soy sauce
    ¼ teaspoon Worcestershire
        sauce
    ¼ teaspoon ground red pepper
    ¼ teaspoon ground nutmeg

Cut off and discard bony wing tips. Cut remaining wings in half. Combine remaining ingredients in large bowl until well blended; add wings. Cover and marinate in refrigerator 1 hour.

Prepare grill. Place wings on grid. Grill 15 to 20 minutes over medium coals, turning frequently.   *Makes 32 appetizers*

Barbecue Beef Ribettes

California Quesadillas

1 small ripe avocado
2 packages (3 ounces each)
   cream cheese, softened
3 tablespoons FRANK'S®
   Original REDHOT®
   Cayenne Pepper Sauce
¼ cup minced fresh cilantro
   leaves
16 (6-inch) flour tortillas
   (2 packages)
1 cup (4 ounces) shredded
   Cheddar or Monterey Jack
   cheese
½ cup finely chopped green
   onions
   Sour cream (optional)

Halve avocado and remove pit. Scoop out flesh into food processor or bowl of electric mixer. Add cream cheese and RedHot® sauce. Cover and process, or beat, until smooth. Add cilantro; process, or beat, until well blended. Spread rounded tablespoon avocado mixture onto each tortilla. Sprinkle half the tortillas with cheese and onions, dividing evenly. Top with remaining tortillas; press gently.

Place tortillas on oiled grid. Grill over medium coals 5 minutes or until cheese melts and tortillas are lightly browned, turning once. Cut into triangles. Serve with sour cream, if desired. Garnish as desired. *Makes 8 appetizer servings*

Note: You may serve avocado mixture as a dip with tortilla chips.

Prep Time: 20 minutes
Cook Time: 5 minutes

Stuffed Portobello Mushrooms

4 portobello mushrooms
   (4 ounces each)
¼ cup olive oil
2 cloves garlic, pressed
6 ounces crumbled goat
   cheese
2 ounces prosciutto or thinly
   sliced ham, chopped
¼ cup chopped fresh basil
   Mixed salad greens

Remove stems and gently scrape gills from underside of mushrooms; discard stems and gills. Brush mushroom caps with combined oil and garlic. Combine cheese, prosciutto and basil in medium bowl. Grill mushrooms, top side up, on covered grill over medium KINGSFORD® Briquets 4 minutes. Turn mushrooms over; fill caps with cheese mixture, dividing equally. Cover and grill 3 to 4 minutes longer until cheese mixture is warm. Remove mushrooms from grill; cut into quarters. Serve on mixed greens. *Makes 4 servings*

California Quesadillas

Sausage-Bacon-Apricot Kabobs

1 package **BOB EVANS®**
   Italian Grillin' Sausage
   (approximately 5 links)
1 cup dried apricot halves
8 slices bacon
3 tablespoons apricot
   preserves
3 tablespoons lemon juice
1 tablespoon Dijon mustard
1 teaspoon Worcestershire
   sauce

Precook sausage 10 minutes in gently boiling water. Drain and cut into ¾-inch slices. Alternate sausage and apricots on 8 wooden skewers,* weaving bacon back and forth in ribbonlike fashion between them. Grill or broil over medium-high heat 3 to 4 minutes on each side. Combine preserves, lemon juice, mustard and Worcestershire in small bowl. Brush preserves mixture on kabobs; continue grilling, turning and basting frequently, until bacon is cooked through. Refrigerate leftovers.   *Makes 8 kabobs*

Soak wooden skewers in water 30 minutes before using to prevent burning.

Thai Chicken Ribbons

½ cup **A.1.®** Steak Sauce
½ cup creamy peanut butter
¼ cup water
2 tablespoons reduced sodium
   soy sauce
2 cloves garlic, minced
2 tablespoons lime juice
2 tablespoons firmly packed
   light brown sugar
½ teaspoon minced fresh
   ginger
½ teaspoon red pepper flakes
1¼ pounds boneless skinless
   chicken breasts, cut
   lengthwise into ½-inch-
   wide strips

In small saucepan, combine steak sauce, peanut butter, water, soy sauce, garlic, lime juice, brown sugar, ginger and red pepper. Over medium heat, cook and stir for 2 to 3 minutes or until smooth.

Soak 12 (10-inch) wooden skewers in water for at least 30 minutes. Thread chicken strips onto skewers. Reserve 1 cup sauce and keep warm for dipping. Grill chicken over medium heat for 6 to 8 minutes or until done, turning and brushing with remaining sauce. Remove from grill; garnish as desired. Serve hot with reserved sauce for dipping.   *Makes 12 appetizers*

Sausage-Bacon-Apricot Kabobs

Savory Herb-Stuffed Onions

1 zucchini, cut lengthwise into
    ¼-inch-thick slices
  Nonstick cooking spray
3 shiitake mushrooms
4 large sweet onions
1 plum tomato, seeded and
    chopped
2 tablespoons fresh bread
    crumbs
1 tablespoon fresh basil *or* 1
    teaspoon dried basil
1 teaspoon olive oil
¼ teaspoon salt
⅛ teaspoon ground black
    pepper
4 teaspoons balsamic vinegar

1. To grill zucchini, spray zucchini on both sides with cooking spray. Grill on uncovered grill over medium coals 4 minutes or until grillmarked and tender, turning once. Cool; cut into bite-size pieces.

2. Thread mushrooms onto metal skewers. Grill on covered grill over medium coals 20 to 30 minutes or until grillmarked and tender. Coarsely chop; set aside.

3. Remove stem and root ends of onions, leaving peels intact. Spray onions with cooking spray; grill root-end up on covered grill over medium coals 5 minutes or until lightly charred. Remove and let stand until cool enough to handle. Peel and scoop about 1 inch of pulp from stem ends; chop for filling and set whole onions aside.

4. Combine chopped onion, mushrooms, zucchini, tomato, bread crumbs, basil, oil, salt and pepper; mix until well blended. Spoon equal amounts of stuffing mixture into centers of onions.

5. Place each onion on sheet of foil; sprinkle each with 1 tablespoon water. Seal using Drugstore Wrap technique (page 5). Grill onion packets on covered grill over medium coals 45 to 60 minutes or until tender. Spoon 1 teaspoon vinegar over each onion before serving.   *Makes 4 appetizer servings*

Savory Herb-Stuffed Onions

Grilled Spiced Halibut, Pineapple and Pepper Skewers

2 tablespoons lemon juice or
 lime juice
1 teaspoon minced garlic
1 teaspoon chili powder
½ teaspoon ground cumin
¼ teaspoon ground cinnamon
⅛ teaspoon ground cloves
½ pound boneless skinless
 halibut steak, about 1 inch
 thick
½ small pineapple, peeled,
 halved lengthwise, cut
 into 24 pieces
1 large green or red bell
 pepper, cut into 24
 squares

1. Combine lemon juice, garlic, chili powder, cumin, cinnamon and cloves in large resealable plastic food storage bag; knead until blended.

2. Rinse fish and pat dry. Cut into 12 cubes about 1 to 1¼ inches square. Add fish to bag; press out air and seal. Turn bag gently to coat fish with marinade. Refrigerate halibut 30 minutes to 1 hour. Soak 12 (6- to 8-inch) bamboo skewers in water while fish marinates.

3. Alternately thread 2 pieces pineapple, 2 pieces pepper and 1 piece fish onto each skewer.

4. Spray cold grid with nonstick cooking spray. Adjust grid 4 to 6 inches above heat. Preheat grill to medium-high heat. Place skewers on grill, cover if possible (or tent with foil) and grill 3 to 4 minutes or until grill marks appear on bottoms. Turn and grill skewers 3 to 4 minutes or until fish is opaque and flakes easily when tested with fork. *Makes 6 servings*

Fiesta Chicken Wings

1 cup A.1.® Steak Sauce
1 cup mild, medium or hot
 thick and chunky salsa
10 chicken wings, split and tips
 remove

In medium bowl, combine steak sauce and salsa; reserve 1 cup for dipping.

In nonmetal bowl, coat wings with remaining sauce. Cover; chill 1 hour, turning occasionally. Grill wings over medium heat for 12 to 15 minutes or until no longer pink, turning occasionally. Serve hot with reserved sauce. *Makes 20 appetizers*

Grilled Spiced Halibut, Pineapple and Pepper Skewers

Turkey Ham Quesadillas

¼ **cup picante sauce or salsa**
4 **(7-inch) regular or whole**
   wheat flour tortillas
½ **cup shredded reduced-**
   sodium reduced-fat
   Monterey Jack cheese
¼ **cup finely chopped turkey**
   ham or lean ham
¼ **cup canned green chilies,**
   drained or 1 to 2
   tablespoons chopped
   fresh jalapeño to taste
Nonstick cooking spray
Additional picante sauce or
   salsa for dipping
   (optional)
Fat-free or low-fat sour
   cream (optional)

1. Spread 1 tablespoon picante sauce on each tortilla.

2. Sprinkle cheese, turkey ham and chilies equally over half of each tortilla; fold over uncovered half to make "sandwich;" spray tops and bottoms of tortilla "sandwiches" with cooking spray.

3. Grill on uncovered grill over medium coals 1½ minutes per side or until cheese is melted and tortillas are golden brown, turning once. Quarter each quesadilla and serve with additional picante sauce and fat-free sour cream, if desired.

Makes 8 appetizer servings

Buffalo-Style Shrimp

⅓ **cup FRANK'S® Original**
   REDHOT® Cayenne
   Pepper Sauce
⅓ **cup butter or margarine,**
   melted
1 **pound raw large shrimp,**
   shelled and deveined
2 **ribs celery, cut into large**
   pieces

1. Combine RedHot® sauce and butter in small bowl. Alternately thread shrimp and celery onto metal skewers. Place in shallow bowl. Pour ⅓ cup RedHot® sauce mixture over kabobs. Cover; refrigerate 30 minutes. Prepare grill.

2. Grill,* over medium coals, 3 to 5 minutes or until shrimp are opaque. Heat remaining RedHot® sauce mixture; pour over shrimp and celery.

Makes 4 servings

*Or, broil 6 inches from heat.

Prep Time: *10 minutes*
Marinate Time: *30 minutes*
Cook Time: *5 minutes*

Turkey Ham Quesadillas

Honeyed Pork and Mango Kabobs

½ cup honey
¼ cup frozen apple juice
    concentrate, thawed
3 tablespoons FRANK'S®
    Original REDHOT®
    Cayenne Pepper Sauce
¼ teaspoon ground allspice
1 teaspoon grated lemon peel
1 pound pork tenderloin, cut
    into 1-inch cubes
1 large (12 ounces) ripe
    mango, peeled, pitted and
    cut into ¾-inch cubes,
    divided
½ cup frozen large baby
    onions, partially thawed

1. Combine honey, juice concentrate, RedHot® sauce and allspice in small saucepan. Bring to a boil over medium heat. Reduce heat to low; cook, stirring, 5 minutes. Stir in lemon peel. Remove from heat. Pour ¼ cup marinade into small bowl; reserve.

2. Place pork in large resealable plastic food storage bag. Pour remaining marinade over pork. Seal bag; refrigerate 1 hour. Prepare grill.

3. To prepare dipping sauce, place ¼ cup mango cubes in blender or food processor. Add reserved ¼ cup marinade. Cover; process until puréed. Transfer to serving bowl; set aside.

4. Alternately thread pork, remaining mango cubes and onions onto metal skewers. Place skewers on oiled grid. Grill*, over medium-low coals, 12 to 15 minutes or until pork is no longer pink. Serve kabobs with dipping sauce.

Makes 6 servings (¾ cup sauce)

*Or, broil 6 inches from heat 10 to 12 minutes or until pork is no longer pink.

Note: You may substitute 1½ cups fresh or frozen peach cubes (2 to 3 peaches) for fresh mango.

Prep Time: *30 minutes*
Marinate Time: *1 hour*
Cook Time: *about 20 minutes*

Honeyed Pork and Mango Kabobs

Sizzling Salads

Thai Beef Salad (page 38)

Grilled Chicken and Melon Salad (page 44)

BLT Chicken Salad for Two

  2 boneless skinless chicken breast halves
¼ cup mayonnaise or salad dressing
½ teaspoon freshly ground black pepper
  4 large leaf lettuce leaves
  I large tomato, seeded and diced
  3 slices crisp-cooked bacon, crumbled
  I hard-cooked egg, sliced
    Additional mayonnaise or salad dressing

1. Brush chicken with mayonnaise; sprinkle with pepper. Grill over hot coals 5 to 7 minutes per side or until no longer pink in center. Cool slightly; cut into thin strips.

2. Arrange lettuce leaves on serving plates. Top with chicken, tomato, bacon and egg. Spoon additional mayonnaise over top. *Makes 2 servings*

Chili-Crusted Grilled Chicken Caesar Salad

1 to 2 lemons
1 tablespoon minced garlic,
    divided
1½ teaspoons dried oregano
    leaves, crushed, divided
1 teaspoon chili powder
1 pound boneless skinless
    chicken breasts
1 tablespoon olive oil
2 anchovy fillets, minced
1 large head romaine lettuce,
    cut into 1-inch strips
¼ cup grated Parmesan
    cheese
4 whole wheat rolls

1. Grate lemon peel; measure 1 to 2 teaspoons. Juice lemon; measure ¼ cup. Combine lemon peel and 1 tablespoon juice in small bowl. Set ¼ teaspoon garlic aside. Add remaining garlic, 1 teaspoon oregano and chili powder to lemon peel mixture; stir to combine. Rub chicken completely with lemon peel mixture.

2. Combine remaining 3 tablespoons lemon juice, reserved ¼ teaspoon garlic, remaining ½ teaspoon oregano, oil and anchovies in large bowl. Add lettuce to bowl; toss to coat with dressing. Sprinkle with cheese; toss.

3. Spray cold grid with nonstick cooking spray. Adjust grid 4 to 6 inches above heat. Preheat grill to medium-high heat. Grill chicken 5 to 6 minutes or until marks are established and surface is dry. Turn chicken over; grill 3 to 4 minutes or until chicken is no longer pink in center.

4. Arrange salad on 4 large plates. Slice chicken. Fan on each salad. Serve with whole wheat rolls. *Makes 4 servings*

Chili-Crusted Grilled Chicken Caesar Salad

Thai Steak Salad with Peanut Dressing

Peanut Dressing (recipe follows)
6 cups washed torn mixed greens
2 ripe mangos, peeled, pitted and sliced
2 cups fresh bean sprouts, rinsed and drained
2 medium tomatoes, cut into wedges
1 medium cucumber, sliced
½ pound thin-cut sirloin tip steak (sandwich steak)
¼ teaspoon ground red pepper or curry powder
Cilantro leaves for garnish

1. Prepare Peanut Dressing; set aside.

2. Arrange greens, mango slices, bean sprouts, tomatoes and cucumber on four plates.

3. Season steak with red pepper. Grill or broil steaks 4 to 6 minutes or until desired doneness, turning halfway through grilling time. Let steak rest 5 minutes on cutting board; cut into strips.

4. Arrange steak on top of prepared plates. Serve with Peanut Dressing; garnish, if desired.

Makes 4 servings

Peanut Dressing

¾ cup creamy peanut butter
½ cup plus 2 tablespoons water
3 tablespoons rice vinegar
2 tablespoons light soy sauce
2 tablespoons molasses
1 tablespoon anchovy paste
2 tablespoons chopped cilantro
2 tablespoons chopped green onion
½ teaspoon ground red pepper

Combine peanut butter, water, vinegar, soy sauce, molasses and anchovy paste in medium bowl with wire whisk until smooth. Stir in cilantro, green onion and red pepper.

Makes about 2 cups

Thai Steak Salad with Peanut Dressing

Grilled Chicken Caesar Salad

1 pound boneless skinless chicken breast halves
½ cup extra-virgin olive oil
3 tablespoons fresh lemon juice
2 teaspoons anchovy paste
2 cloves garlic, minced
½ teaspoon salt
½ teaspoon pepper
6 cups torn romaine lettuce leaves
4 plum tomatoes, quartered
¼ cup grated Parmesan cheese
1 cup purchased garlic croutons
Anchovy fillets (optional)
Additional pepper (optional)

1. Place chicken in large resealable plastic food storage bag. Combine oil, lemon juice, anchovy paste, garlic, salt and ½ teaspoon pepper in small bowl. Reserve ⅓ cup of marinade; cover and refrigerate until serving. Pour remaining marinade over chicken in bag. Seal bag tightly, turning to coat. Marinate in refrigerator at least 1 hour or up to 4 hours, turning occasionally.

2. Combine lettuce, tomatoes and cheese in large bowl. Cover; refrigerate until serving.

3. Prepare barbecue grill for direct cooking.

4. Drain chicken; reserve marinade from bag. Place chicken on grid. Grill chicken, on covered grill, over medium coals 10 to 12 minutes or until chicken is no longer pink in center, brushing with reserved marinade from bag after 5 minutes and turning halfway through grilling time. Discard remaining marinade from bag. Cool chicken slightly.

5. Slice warm chicken crosswise into ½-inch-wide strips; add chicken and croutons to lettuce mixture in bowl. Drizzle with ⅓ cup reserved marinade; toss to coat well. Top with anchovy fillets and serve with additional pepper.   *Makes 4 servings*

Note: Chicken may also be refrigerated until cold before slicing.

Grilled Chicken Caesar Salad

Grilled Chicken Salad with Avocado Dressing

1 cup vegetable oil
⅓ cup GREY POUPON® Dijon Mustard
¼ cup red wine vinegar
2 tablespoons lime juice
2 tablespoons chopped cilantro or parsley
¼ teaspoon dried oregano leaves
⅛ teaspoon ground red pepper
6 boneless, skinless chicken breasts (about 1½ pounds)
1 ripe medium avocado, pitted and peeled
6 cups torn salad greens
1 large tomato, cut into wedges

In small bowl, whisk oil, mustard, vinegar, lime juice, cilantro or parsley, oregano and pepper until blended. Reserve 1 cup mustard mixture. In nonmetal dish, combine remaining mustard mixture and chicken. Cover; chill for at least 2 hours.

In blender or food processor, blend avocado and 1 cup reserved mustard mixture until smooth. Cover; chill until serving time.

Remove chicken from marinade, reserving marinade. Grill or broil chicken 6 inches from heat source for 10 to 15 minutes or until done, turning and brushing with marinade occasionally. Slice chicken on a diagonal. Serve chicken on salad greens; top with tomato and avocado dressing. *Makes 6 servings*

Hot Off The Grill

After food is removed from a marinade, the marinade may be used as a basting or dipping sauce. When using as a basting sauce, it should only be applied up to the last 5 minutes of grilling. This precaution is necessary because the marinade could have become contaminated with harmful bacteria from the raw food during the marinading process.

Blackened Chicken Salad

2 cups cubed sourdough or
   French bread
  Nonstick cooking spray
1 tablespoon paprika
1 teaspoon onion powder
1 teaspoon garlic powder
½ teaspoon dried oregano
   leaves
½ teaspoon dried thyme leaves
½ teaspoon white pepper
½ teaspoon ground red pepper
½ teaspoon black pepper
1 pound boneless skinless
   chicken breasts
4 cups bite-size pieces fresh
   spinach leaves
2 cups bite-size pieces
   romaine lettuce
2 cups cubed zucchini
2 cups cubed seeded
   cucumber
½ cup sliced green onions with
   tops
1 medium tomato, cut into
   8 wedges
  Ranch Salad Dressing
   (recipe follows)

1. Preheat oven to 375°F. To make croutons, spray bread cubes lightly with cooking spray; place in 15×10-inch jelly-roll pan. Bake 10 to 15 minutes or until browned, stirring occasionally.

2. Combine paprika, onion powder, garlic powder, oregano, thyme, white pepper, red pepper and black pepper in small bowl; rub on all surfaces of chicken. Broil chicken, 6 inches from heat source, 7 to 8 minutes on each side or until chicken is no longer pink in center. Or, grill chicken on covered grill over medium-hot coals, 10 minutes on each side or until chicken is no longer pink in center. Cool slightly. Cut chicken into thin strips.

3. Combine warm chicken, greens, zucchini, cucumber, green onions, tomato and croutons in large bowl. Drizzle with Ranch Salad Dressing; toss to coat. Serve immediately.

Makes 4 servings

Ranch Salad Dressing

  ¼ cup water
  3 tablespoons reduced-calorie cucumber-ranch salad
    dressing
  1 tablespoon reduced-fat mayonnaise or salad dressing
  1 tablespoon lemon juice
  2 teaspoons minced fresh parsley
  ⅛ teaspoon salt
  ⅛ teaspoon pepper

1. In small jar with tight-fitting lid, combine all ingredients; shake well. Refrigerate until ready to use; shake before using.

Makes about ½ cup

Grilled Chicken au Poivre Salad

4 boneless skinless chicken breast halves (about 1¼ pounds)
¼ cup plus 3 tablespoons olive oil, divided
¼ cup finely chopped onion
3 cloves garlic, minced
2½ tablespoons white wine vinegar, divided
2 teaspoons cracked or coarse ground black pepper
½ teaspoon salt
¼ teaspoon poultry seasoning
1 tablespoon Dijon mustard
Dash sugar
1 bag (10 ounces) salad greens
4 cherry tomatoes

Place chicken, ¼ cup oil, onion, garlic, 1 tablespoon vinegar, pepper, salt and poultry seasoning in resealable plastic food storage bag. Seal bag; knead to coat chicken. Refrigerate at least 2 hours or overnight.

Grill chicken, on covered grill, over medium-hot coals 10 to 15 minutes or until chicken is no longer pink in center.

For dressing, combine remaining 3 tablespoons oil, 1½ tablespoons vinegar, mustard and sugar in small bowl; whisk until smooth.

Arrange salad greens and cherry tomatoes on 4 plates.

Cut chicken crosswise into strips. Arrange strips on top of greens. Drizzle with dressing.   *Makes 4 servings*

Wilted Steak Salad

½ cup A.1.® Steak Sauce
⅓ cup red wine vinegar
¼ cup vegetable oil
1 (1-pound) beef top round steak
6 cups torn mixed salad greens
1 cup cherry tomato halves
½ cup sliced cucumber
¼ cup crumbled blue cheese, optional

In small bowl, blend steak sauce, vinegar and oil. Place steak in glass dish; coat with ¼ cup steak sauce mixture. Cover; chill 1 hour, turning occasionally.

In small saucepan, over medium heat, heat remaining steak sauce mixture to a boil; reduce heat and simmer 1 minute. Keep warm.

Remove steak from marinade. Grill over medium heat for 6 minutes on each side or until done. Cut steak into thin slices. In salad bowl, arrange salad greens, steak, tomatoes and cucumber. Pour warm marinade over salad; top with blue cheese if desired. Toss to coat well; serve immediately.   *Makes 6 servings*

Grilled Chicken au Poivre Salad

Thai Beef Salad

Dressing
- 1 cup packed fresh mint or basil leaves, coarsely chopped
- 1 cup olive-oil vinaigrette dressing
- ⅓ cup **FRANK'S**® Original **REDHOT**® Cayenne Pepper Sauce
- 3 tablespoons chopped peeled fresh ginger
- 3 tablespoons sugar
- 3 cloves garlic, chopped
- 2 teaspoons **FRENCH'S**® Worcestershire Sauce

Salad
- 1 flank steak (about 1½ pounds)
- 6 cups washed and torn mixed salad greens
- 1 cup sliced peeled cucumber
- ⅓ cup chopped peanuts

1. Place Dressing ingredients in blender or food processor. Cover; process until smooth. Reserve 1 cup Dressing.

2. Place steak in large resealable plastic food storage bag. Pour remaining Dressing over steak. Seal bag; refrigerate 30 minutes.

3. Prepare grill. Place steak on grid, reserving marinade. Grill, over hot coals, about 15 minutes for medium-rare, brushing frequently with marinade. Let stand 5 minutes. Slice steak diagonally and arrange over salad greens and cucumber.

4. Sprinkle with peanuts and drizzle with reserved 1 cup Dressing. Serve warm. *Makes 6 servings*

Hot Off The Grill

Cleanup is easier if the grill rack is coated with vegetable oil or nonstick cooking spray before grilling.

Thai Beef Salad

Sausage & Wilted Spinach Salad

¼ cup sherry vinegar or white
    wine vinegar
1 teaspoon whole mustard
    seeds, crushed
½ teaspoon salt
¼ teaspoon black pepper
2 ears corn, husked
1 large red onion, cut into
    ¾-inch-thick slices
4 tablespoons extra-virgin
    olive oil, divided
12 ounces smoked turkey,
    chicken or pork sausage
    links, such as Polish,
    Andouille or New Mexico
    style, cut in half
    lengthwise
2 cloves garlic, minced
10 cups lightly packed spinach
    leaves, torn
1 large avocado, peeled and
    cubed

Combine vinegar, mustard seeds, salt and pepper; set dressing aside. Brush corn and onion with 1 tablespoon oil. Insert wooden picks into onion slices from edges to prevent separating into rings. (Soak wooden picks in hot water 15 minutes to prevent burning.) Grill sausage, corn and onion over medium KINGSFORD® Briquets 6 to 10 minutes until vegetables are crisp-tender and sausage is hot, turning several times. Cut corn kernels from cobs; chop onion and slice sausage. Heat remaining 3 tablespoons oil in small skillet over medium heat. Add garlic; cook and stir 1 minute. Toss spinach, avocado, sausage, corn, onion and dressing in large bowl. Drizzle hot oil over salad; toss and serve immediately.

Makes 4 servings

Hot Off The Grill

To check the temperature of the coals, cautiously hold the palm of your hand at grid level—over the coals for direct heat—and count the number of seconds you can hold your hand in that position before the heat forces you to pull away. For a medium grill (about 300°F to 350°F, you should be able to hold your hand there for 4 seconds.

Sausage & Wilted Spinach Salad

Fajita-Style Beef Salad

¾ **pound top sirloin steak**
1 **package (1.0 ounce)**
   LAWRY'S® Taco Spices &
   Seasonings
½ **cup water**
¼ **teaspoon hot pepper sauce**
1 **quart salad greens, torn into**
   bite-size pieces
1 **green bell pepper, chopped**
1 **onion, thinly sliced**
½ **cup shredded red cabbage**
1 **can (8¾ ounces) garbanzo**
   beans, drained
1 **tomato, cut into wedges**
   Tortilla chips

Spicy Tomato Vinaigrette
   1 **cup prepared chunky salsa**
   ½ **cup vegetable oil**
   ¼ **cup white wine vinegar**
   2 **tablespoons sliced green**
      onion, including tops
   ½ **teaspoon sugar**
   ½ **teaspoon LAWRY'S® Garlic**
      Salt
   ½ **teaspoon LAWRY'S®**
      Seasoned Pepper

Pierce steak several times on each side; place in large resealable plastic food storage bag. In small bowl, combine Taco Spices & Seasonings, water and hot pepper sauce; blend well. Pour marinade over steak, seal bag and refrigerate 30 minutes or overnight. Grill or broil steak 10 to 12 minutes, or until desired doneness, turning once and basting often with marinade. *Do not baste during last 5 minutes of cooking.* Slice into thin strips. In large bowl, toss together salad greens, green pepper, onion, cabbage and garbanzo beans. Place on individual plates or serving platter. Top with beef strips, tomato wedges and tortilla chips. Serve with Spicy Tomato Vinaigrette. *Makes 6 side-dish or 4 main-dish servings*

Spicy Tomato Vinaigrette: In container with stopper or lid, combine all ingredients. Seal top and shake vigorously to blend well. Chill.

Serving Suggestion: Serve over salad or on the side.

Hint: For a smoother texture, quickly mix in blender or food processor.

Grilled Chicken and Spiced Melon Salad

1 medium (2½ to 3 pounds)
    cantaloupe
1 large (4 to 4½ pounds)
    honeydew
½ cup lime juice, divided
3 tablespoons chopped fresh
    mint or basil leaves
1 jalapeño pepper,* stemmed,
    seeded, minced
2 tablespoons honey, divided
1 tablespoon minced fresh
    ginger
2 teaspoons finely minced
    garlic
1 teaspoon coarsely ground
    black pepper
1½ pounds chicken tenders

*Jalapeño peppers can sting and irritate the skin; wear rubber gloves when handling peppers and do not touch eyes. Wash hands after handling peppers.

1. Cover 12 bamboo skewers with water and let soak at least 30 minutes. Cut melons in half; scoop out and discard seeds. Cut cantaloupe into 18 wedges. Cut off and discard rind. Place wedges in resealable plastic food storage bag; set aside. Scoop out balls of honeydew with melon baller. Place in bag with wedges. Combine ¼ cup lime juice, mint, jalapeño, 1 tablespoon honey and ginger in small bowl; pour into bag. Seal bag and gently turn to evenly coat melon. Refrigerate while preparing meat.

2. Combine remaining ¼ cup lime juice, remaining 1 tablespoon honey, garlic and black pepper in medium bowl. Thread chicken onto skewers. Place skewers on rimmed baking pan and brush both sides generously with marinade. Just before placing chicken on grill, drain melon, reserving dressing. Fan wedges on 6 plates. Spoon melon balls at base of each fan. Drizzle servings with dressing.

3. Prepare coals for grilling. Place chicken on grid, 3 to 4 inches from medium coals. Grill 5 to 7 minutes or until no longer pink in center, turning occasionally. Lay 2 skewers on each plate of melon.

Makes 6 servings

Grilled Chicken and Melon Salad

¾ cup orange marmalade, divided
¼ cup plus 2 tablespoons white wine vinegar, divided
2 tablespoons low-sodium soy sauce
1 tablespoon grated fresh ginger
4 boneless skinless chicken breast halves
½ cantaloupe, peeled, seeded and sliced
½ honeydew melon, peeled, seeded and cut into 1-inch-thick slices
2 tablespoons olive oil
2 tablespoons minced fresh cilantro
1 teaspoon jalapeño pepper sauce
10 cups mixed lettuce greens
1 pint fresh strawberries, halved

1. Combine ⅓ cup orange marmalade, 2 tablespoons vinegar, soy sauce and ginger. Brush marmalade mixture over chicken and melons. Arrange melons in grill basket or thread onto skewers.

2. Grill chicken over hot coals 5 to 7 minutes on each side or until no longer pink in center. Grill melons, covered, 2 to 3 minutes on each side. Refrigerate overnight.

3. Combine remaining marmalade, ¼ cup vinegar, oil, cilantro and jalapeño pepper sauce in jar with tight-fitting lid; shake well to blend.

4. To complete recipe, arrange lettuce, chicken, melon and strawberries on serving plates; spoon marmalade mixture over top.

Makes 4 servings

Tip: For a special touch, garnish with fresh produce such as red and green bell peppers or jalapeño peppers.

Make-Ahead Time: *Up to 1 day before serving*
Final Prep Time: *5 minutes*

Grilled Chicken and Melon Salad

Salmon, Asparagus and Shiitake Salad

¼ cup cider vinegar
¼ cup extra-virgin olive oil
  Grated peel and juice of 1
    lemon
4 teaspoons Dijon mustard,
    divided
1 clove garlic, minced
¼ teaspoon salt
¼ teaspoon black pepper
2 teaspoons minced fresh
    tarragon or ¾ teaspoon
    dried tarragon leaves
1 pound small salmon fillets,
    skinned
1 medium red onion, thinly
    sliced
1 pound asparagus, ends
    trimmed
¼ pound shiitake mushrooms
    or button mushrooms
  Additional salt and black
    pepper
8 cups lightly packed torn
    romaine and red leaf
    lettuce

Combine vinegar, oil, peel, juice, 2 teaspoons mustard, garlic, ¼ teaspoon salt and ¼ teaspoon pepper in medium bowl; spoon 3 tablespoons dressing into 2-quart glass dish to use as marinade. Reserve remaining dressing. Add tarragon and 2 teaspoons remaining mustard to marinade in glass dish; blend well. Add salmon; turn to coat. Cover and refrigerate 1 hour. Transfer 3 tablespoons of reserved dressing to medium bowl; add onion, tossing to coat. Thread asparagus and mushrooms onto wooden skewers. (Soak skewers in hot water 30 minutes to prevent burning.)

Remove salmon from marinade; discard marinade. Season salmon to taste with additional salt and pepper. Lightly oil hot grid to prevent sticking. Grill salmon over medium-hot KINGSFORD® Briquets 2 to 4 minutes per side until fish flakes when tested with fork. Grill asparagus and mushrooms over medium-hot briquets 5 to 8 minutes until crisp-tender. Cut asparagus into 2-inch pieces and slice mushrooms; add to onion mixture. Let stand 10 minutes. Toss lettuce with onion mixture in large bowl; arrange lettuce on platter. Break salmon into 2-inch pieces; arrange salmon and vegetables over lettuce. Drizzle with remaining reserved dressing. Serve immediately. *Makes 4 main-dish servings*

Salmon, Asparagus and Shiitake Salad

Flank Steak Salad with Wine-Mustard Dressing

1 flank steak (about 1½
    pounds) *or* 3½ cups thinly
    sliced cooked roast beef
2 tablespoons white wine
    vinegar
1 tablespoon Dijon mustard
½ teaspoon **LAWRY'S**®
    Seasoned Pepper
6 tablespoons vegetable oil
1 pound small red potatoes,
    cooked and sliced
½ pound fresh green beans,
    steamed until tender-crisp
1 jar (6 ounces) marinated
    artichoke hearts, drained
¼ pound mushrooms, sliced
5 green onions including tops,
    sliced

Grill or broil steak 10 to 12 minutes or until desired doneness, turning halfway through grilling time. In small bowl, combine vinegar, mustard and Seasoned Pepper; mix with wire whisk. Slowly add oil, beating constantly. Thinly slice steak on the diagonal across the grain. Cut each slice into 2-inch strips. Place in large salad bowl; add dressing and toss gently. Add remaining ingredients and toss. Serve at room temperature. *Makes 6 to 8 servings*

Serving Suggestion: Arrange bed of lettuce on individual plates and serve steak and vegetable mixture on top.

Hint: For extra flavor, marinate steak in Lawry's® Seasoned Marinade or Dijon & Honey Marinade with Lemon Juice.

Hot Off The Grill

Marinades add unique flavors to foods and help tenderize less-tender cuts of meats. Turn marinating foods occasionally to let the flavor infuse evenly. Heavy-duty plastic bags are great to hold foods as they marinate.

Flank Steak Salad with Wine-Mustard Dressing

Grilled Chicken Salad with Creamy Tarragon Dressing

Creamy Tarragon Dressing (recipe follows)
1 pound chicken tenders
1 teaspoon Cajun or Creole seasoning
1 package (10 ounces) prepared mixed salad greens
2 apples, thinly sliced
1 cup packed alfalfa sprouts
2 tablespoons raisins

1. Prepare Creamy Tarragon Dressing.

2. Season chicken with Cajun seasoning. To prevent sticking, spray grid with nonstick cooking spray. Prepare grill for direct cooking. Place chicken on grid, 3 to 4 inches from medium-high coals. Grill 5 to 7 minutes on each side or until no longer pink in center.

3. Divide salad greens among 4 large plates. Arrange chicken, apples and sprouts on top of greens. Sprinkle raisins on top and garnish with sprigs of tarragon, if desired. Serve with dressing.

Makes 4 servings

Prep Time: *10 minutes*
Cook Time: *14 minutes*

Creamy Tarragon Dressing
½ cup plain nonfat yogurt
¼ cup low-fat sour cream
¼ cup frozen apple juice concentrate, thawed
1 tablespoon spicy brown mustard
1 tablespoon minced fresh tarragon leaves

1. Combine all ingredients in small bowl.

Makes about 1 cup

Grilled Pesto Steak 'n' Vegetable Salad

**½ cup A.1.® Original or A.1.®
Bold & Spicy Steak Sauce**
¼ cup lemon juice
3 tablespoons purchased
pesto
3 tablespoons chopped fresh
parsley
2 teaspoons grated lemon
peel
½ cup olive oil
1 medium Italian eggplant, cut
crosswise into 8 slices
1 medium zucchini, cut
crosswise into 8 slices
1 medium yellow squash, cut
crosswise into 8 slices
1 large red bell pepper, cut
into 8 wedges
1 (1-pound) beef top round
steak, about 1 inch thick
4 cups torn mixed salad
greens

In small bowl, blend steak sauce, juice, pesto, parsley and lemon peel; slowly whisk in oil until well blended. Place vegetables and steak in separate nonmetal dishes; coat each with ⅓ cup steak sauce mixture. Cover; refrigerate 1 hour, turning occasionally. Reserve remaining steak sauce mixture for dressing.

Remove steak and vegetables from marinades; reserve marinades separately for basting. Grill steak over medium heat 6 minutes on each side or to desired doneness, basting with marinade from steak. Grill vegetables over medium-high heat 2 to 3 minutes on each side or until tender-crisp, basting with marinade from vegetables. (Discard any remaining marinade.) Heat reserved dressing mixture until warm. Arrange salad greens on serving platter. Thinly slice steak; arrange steak and vegetables on salad greens. Serve immediately with warm dressing.

Makes 4 servings

Grilled Chicken Caesar Salad

1 pound boneless skinless chicken breast halves
3 tablespoons lemon juice
2 tablespoons olive oil
1 teaspoon dried oregano leaves

Creamy Caesar Salad Dressing
¼ cup sour cream
3 tablespoons olive oil
1 tablespoon lemon juice
1 teaspoon FRENCH'S® Worcestershire Sauce
½ teaspoon anchovy paste (optional)
¼ teaspoon cracked black pepper
¼ cup grated Parmesan cheese

Salad
8 cups assorted lettuce greens, washed
1⅓ cups FRENCH'S® French Fried Onions

Place chicken, 3 tablespoons lemon juice, 2 tablespoons oil and oregano in resealable plastic food storage bag. Marinate chicken in refrigerator 15 minutes.

Grill or broil chicken 10 minutes or until no longer pink in center, turning halfway through cooking time. Cover; set aside.

To prepare Creamy Caesar Salad Dressing, combine dressing ingredients in blender or food processor. Cover; process until smooth. Set aside.

To serve, arrange salad greens on 4 dinner plates. Slice chicken diagonally and arrange over lettuce. Microwave French Fried Onions in microwavable bowl on HIGH 1 minute or until golden. Sprinkle over chicken and lettuce. Serve with Creamy Caesar Salad Dressing.   *Makes 4 servings (about ¾ cup dressing)*

Prep Time: *20 minutes*
Marinate Time: *15 minutes*
Cook Time: *10 minutes*

Grilled Chicken Caesar Salad

Burger Bonanza & More

Caramelized Onion & Eggplant Sandwich (page 100)

Grilled Chicken & Fresh Salsa Wrap (page 116)

Dijon Bacon Cheeseburgers

1 cup shredded Cheddar cheese (4 ounces)
5 tablespoons **GREY POUPON®** Dijon Mustard,*
   divided
2 teaspoons dried minced onion
1 teaspoon prepared horseradish*
1 pound lean ground beef
4 onion sandwich rolls, split and toasted
1 cup shredded lettuce
4 slices tomato
4 slices bacon, cooked and halved

*5 tablespoons GREY POUPON® Horseradish Mustard may be substituted
for Dijon mustard; omit horseradish.

In small bowl, combine cheese, 3 tablespoons mustard,
onion and horseradish; set aside.

In medium bowl, combine ground beef and remaining
mustard; shape mixture into 4 patties. Grill or broil burgers
over medium heat for 5 minutes on each side or until
desired doneness; top with cheese mixture and cook until
cheese melts, about 2 minutes. Top each roll bottom with
1/4 cup shredded lettuce, 1 tomato slice, burger, 2 bacon
pieces and roll top. Serve immediately.

Makes 4 burgers

Blue Cheese Burgers

1¼ pounds lean ground beef
1 tablespoon finely chopped onion
1½ teaspoons chopped fresh thyme *or* ½ teaspoon dried thyme leaves
¾ teaspoon salt
Dash ground pepper
4 ounces blue cheese, crumbled

Preheat grill.

Combine ground beef, onion, thyme, salt and pepper in medium bowl; mix lightly. Shape into eight patties.

Place cheese in center of four patties to within ½ inch of outer edge; top with remaining burgers. Press edges together to seal.

Grill 8 minutes or to desired doneness, turning once. Serve with lettuce, tomatoes and Dijon mustard on whole wheat buns, if desired.

Makes 4 servings

Burgers Canadian

½ cup mayonnaise
½ cup A.1.® Original or A.1.® Bold & Spicy Steak Sauce, divided
2 tablespoons prepared horseradish
1 pound ground beef
2 ounces Cheddar cheese, sliced
4 slices Canadian bacon (about 4 ounces)
4 sesame sandwich rolls, split, lightly toasted
4 curly lettuce leaves

In small bowl, combine mayonnaise, 6 tablespoons steak sauce and horseradish. Cover; refrigerate at least 1 hour or up to 2 days.

Shape beef into 4 patties. Grill burgers over medium heat or broil 6 inches from heat source 4 minutes on each side or until no longer pink in center, basting with remaining 2 tablespoons steak sauce. When almost done, top each with 1 cheese slice; grill until cheese melts. Grill bacon 1 minute on each side or until heated through. Spread 2 tablespoons chilled sauce on each roll bottom; top each with burger, warm bacon slice, lettuce leaf and roll top. Serve immediately with remaining chilled sauce for dipping.

Makes 4 servings

Blue Cheese Burger

Greek Lamb Burgers

¼ cup pine nuts
1 pound lean ground lamb
¼ cup finely chopped onion
3 cloves garlic, minced, divided
¾ teaspoon salt
¼ teaspoon black pepper
¼ cup plain yogurt
¼ teaspoon sugar
4 slices red onion (¼ inch thick)
1 tablespoon olive oil
8 pumpernickel bread slices
12 thin cucumber slices
4 tomato slices

Prepare grill for direct cooking. Meanwhile, heat small skillet over medium heat until hot. Add pine nuts; cook 30 to 45 seconds until light brown, shaking pan occasionally.

Combine lamb, pine nuts, chopped onion, 2 cloves garlic, salt and pepper in large bowl; mix well. Shape mixture into 4 patties, about ½ inch thick and 4 inches in diameter. Combine yogurt, sugar and remaining 1 clove garlic in small bowl; set aside.

Brush 1 side of each patty and onion slice with oil; place on grid, oil sides down. Brush other sides with oil. Grill, on covered grill, over medium-hot coals 8 to 10 minutes for medium or to desired doneness, turning halfway through grilling time. Place bread on grid to toast during last few minutes of grilling time; grill 1 to 2 minutes per side.

Top 4 bread slices with patties and onion slices; top each with 3 cucumber slices and 1 tomato slice. Dollop evenly with yogurt mixture. Top sandwiches with remaining 4 bread slices. Serve immediately.

Makes 4 servings

Nutty Burgers

1½ pounds ground beef
1 medium onion, finely chopped
1 cup dry bread crumbs
⅔ cup pine nuts
⅓ cup grated Parmesan cheese
⅓ cup chopped fresh parsley
2 eggs
1½ teaspoons salt
1 teaspoon pepper
1 clove garlic, finely chopped

Combine all ingredients; blend well. Shape into 6 thick patties. Grill patties, on covered grill, over medium-hot KINGSFORD® Briquets 5 minutes on each side or until desired doneness.

Makes 6 servings

Greek Lamb Burger

Southwest Pesto Burgers

Cilantro Pesto
1 large clove garlic
4 ounces fresh cilantro, stems removed and rinsed
1½ teaspoons bottled minced jalapeño pepper or 1 tablespoon bottled sliced jalapeño pepper, drained
¼ teaspoon salt
¼ cup vegetable oil

Burgers
1¼ pounds ground beef
¼ cup plus 1 tablespoon Cilantro Pesto, divided
½ teaspoon salt
4 slices pepper Jack cheese
2 tablespoons light or regular mayonnaise
4 kaiser rolls, split
1 ripe avocado, peeled and sliced
Salsa

1. For pesto, with motor running, drop garlic through feed tube of food processor; process until minced. Add cilantro, jalapeño pepper and salt; process until cilantro is chopped.

2. With motor running, slowly add oil through feed tube; process until thick paste forms. Transfer to container with tight-fitting lid. Store in refrigerator up to 3 weeks.

3. To complete recipe, prepare barbecue grill for direct cooking.

4. Combine beef, ¼ cup pesto and salt in large bowl; mix well. Form into 4 patties. Place patties on grid over medium-hot coals. Grill, uncovered, 4 to 5 minutes per side or until meat is no longer pink in center. Add cheese to patties during last 1 minute of grilling.

5. While patties are cooking, combine mayonnaise and remaining 1 tablespoon pesto in small bowl; mix well. Top patties with mayonnaise mixture. Serve on rolls with avocado and salsa.

Makes 4 servings

Serving Suggestion: Serve with nachos or refried beans.

Make-Ahead Time: up to 3 weeks in refrigerator
Final Prep and Cook Time: 20 minutes

Southwest Pesto Burger

California Turkey Burgers

1 pound ground turkey
½ cup finely chopped cilantro
⅓ cup plain dry bread crumbs
**3 tablespoons FRENCH'S®
     Classic Yellow® Mustard**
1 egg, beaten
½ teaspoon salt
¼ teaspoon black pepper
**8 thin slices (3 ounces)
     Monterey Jack cheese**
**½ red or yellow bell pepper,
     seeded and cut into rings**
4 hamburger buns

1. Combine turkey, cilantro, bread crumbs, mustard, egg, salt and pepper in large bowl. Shape into 4 patties, pressing firmly.

2. Place patties on oiled grid. Grill over high heat 15 minutes or until no longer pink in center. Top burgers with cheese during last few minutes of grilling. Grill pepper rings 2 minutes. To serve, place burgers on buns and top with pepper rings. Serve with additional mustard, if desired.   *Makes 4 servings*

Prep Time: *15 minutes*
Cook Time: *15 minutes*

Bacon Burgers

1 pound lean ground beef
**4 crisply cooked bacon slices,
     crumbled**
**1½ teaspoons chopped fresh
     thyme or ½ teaspoon
     dried thyme leaves**
½ teaspoon salt
**   Dash freshly ground pepper**
4 slices Swiss cheese

Preheat grill.

Combine ground beef, bacon, thyme, salt and pepper in medium bowl; mix lightly. Shape into four patties.

Grill 4 minutes; turn. Top with cheese. Continue grilling 2 minutes or to desired doneness.   *Makes 4 servings*

California Turkey Burger

Curried Walnut Grain Burgers

2 eggs
⅓ cup plain yogurt
2 teaspoons Worcestershire
    sauce
2 teaspoons curry powder
½ teaspoon salt
¼ teaspoon ground red pepper
1⅓ cups cooked couscous or
    brown rice
½ cup finely chopped walnuts
½ cup grated carrot
½ cup minced green onions
⅓ cup fine, dry plain bread
    crumbs
4 sesame seed hamburger
    buns
    Honey mustard
    Thinly sliced cucumber or
    apple
    Alfalfa sprouts

1. Combine eggs, yogurt, Worcestershire sauce, curry, salt and red pepper in large bowl; beat until blended. Stir in couscous, walnuts, carrot, green onions and bread crumbs. Shape into 4 (1-inch-thick) patties.

2. Coat grill rack with nonstick cooking spray; place rack on grill over medium-hot coals (350° to 400°F). Place burgers on rack and grill 5 to 6 minutes per side or until done. Serve on buns with mustard, cucumber and sprouts.

Makes 4 servings

Note: Burgers may be broiled 4 inches from heat source for 5 to 6 minutes per side or until done.

Prep and Cook Time: *25 minutes*

Hot Off The Grill

This great meatless burger is a wonderful alternative to the traditional hamburger. Serve it with fresh fruit and carrot sticks for an award-winning meal.

Curried Walnut Grain Burger

Fresh Rockfish Burgers

**8 ounces skinless rockfish or
   scrod fillet**
**1 egg white or 2 tablespoons
   egg substitute**
¼ cup dry bread crumbs
1 green onion, finely chopped
**1 tablespoon finely chopped
   parsley**
2 teaspoons fresh lime juice
1½ teaspoons capers
1 teaspoon Dijon mustard
¼ teaspoon salt
**⅛ teaspoon black pepper
   Nonstick cooking spray**
**4 grilled whole wheat English
   muffins**
4 leaf lettuce leaves
**4 slices red or yellow tomato
   Additional Dijon mustard
   for serving, if desired**

1. Finely chop rockfish and place in medium bowl. Add egg white, bread crumbs, onion, parsley, lime juice, capers, mustard, salt and pepper; gently combine with fork. Shape into 4 patties.

2. Spray heavy grillproof cast iron skillet or griddle with nonstick cooking spray; place on grid over hot coals to heat. Spray tops of burgers with additional cooking spray. Place burgers in hot skillet; grill on covered grill over hot coals 4 to 5 minutes or until burgers are browned on both sides, turning once. Serve on English muffins or buns with lettuce, tomato slice and Dijon mustard, if desired.

Makes 4 servings

Blackened Burgers

1 pound ground beef
**5 tablespoons A.1.® Steak
   Sauce, divided**
**4 teaspoons coarsely cracked
   black pepper, divided**
4 kaiser rolls, split
4 tomato slices

In medium bowl, combine ground beef, 3 tablespoons steak sauce and 1 teaspoon pepper; shape mixture into 4 patties. Brush patties with remaining steak sauce; coat with remaining pepper.

Grill burgers over medium heat for 5 minutes on each side or until done. Top each roll bottom with burger, tomato slice and roll top. Serve immediately.

Makes 4 servings

Fresh Rockfish Burger

Greek Burgers

**Yogurt Sauce (recipe
  follows)**
1 pound ground beef
2 tablespoons red wine
**1 tablespoon chopped fresh
  oregano *or* 1 teaspoon
  dried oregano leaves**
2 teaspoons ground cumin
½ teaspoon salt
Dash ground red pepper
Dash black pepper
Pita bread
Lettuce
Chopped tomatoes

Prepare Yogurt Sauce.

Soak 4 bamboo skewers in water. Combine ground beef, wine, oregano, cumin, salt, red pepper and black pepper in medium bowl; mix lightly. Divide mixture into eight equal portions; form each portion into an oval, each about 4 inches long. Cover; chill 30 minutes.

Preheat grill. Insert skewers lengthwise through centers of ovals, placing 2 on each skewer. Grill about 8 minutes or to desired doneness, turning once. Fill pita bread with lettuce, meat and chopped tomatoes. Serve with Yogurt Sauce.   *Makes 4 servings*

Yogurt Sauce

2 cups plain yogurt
1 cup chopped red onion
1 cup chopped cucumber
**¼ cup chopped fresh mint *or* 1 tablespoon plus 1½
  teaspoons dried mint leaves**
**1 tablespoon chopped fresh marjoram *or* 1 teaspoon
  dried marjoram leaves**

Combine ingredients in small bowl. Cover; chill up to 4 hours before serving.

Greek Burgers

Blue Cheese Burgers with Red Onion

2 pounds ground chuck
2 cloves garlic, minced
1 teaspoon salt
½ teaspoon black pepper
4 ounces blue cheese
⅓ cup coarsely chopped
    walnuts, toasted
1 torpedo (long) red onion *or*
    2 small red onions, sliced
    into ⅜-inch-thick rounds
2 baguettes (each 12 inches
    long)
    Olive or vegetable oil

Combine beef, garlic, salt and pepper in medium bowl. Shape meat mixture into 12 oval patties. Mash cheese and blend with walnuts in small bowl. Divide cheese mixture equally; place onto centers of 6 meat patties. Top with remaining meat patties; tightly pinch edges together to seal in filling.

Oil hot grid to help prevent sticking. Grill patties and onion, if desired, on covered grill, over medium KINGSFORD® Briquets, 7 to 12 minutes for medium doneness, turning once. Cut baguettes into 4-inch lengths; split each piece and brush cut side with olive oil. Move cooked burgers to edge of grill to keep warm. Grill bread, oil side down, until lightly toasted. Serve burgers on toasted baguettes.

Makes 6 servings

Backyard Burgers

1½ pounds ground beef
⅓ cup barbecue sauce, divided
2 tablespoons finely chopped
    onion
½ teaspoon dried oregano
    leaves, crushed
6 onion hamburger buns, split
    and toasted

1. In large bowl, combine ground beef, 2 tablespoons barbecue sauce, onion and oregano. Shape into six 1-inch-thick patties.

2. Place patties on grill rack directly above medium coals. Grill, uncovered, until desired doneness, turning and brushing often with remaining barbecue sauce. To serve, place patties on buns.

Makes 6 servings

Blue Cheese Burger with Red Onion

Grilled Feta Burgers

½ pound lean ground sirloin
½ pound ground turkey breast
2 teaspoons grated lemon peel
1 teaspoon olive oil
1 teaspoon dried oregano leaves
¼ teaspoon salt
⅛ teaspoon ground black pepper
1 ounce feta cheese
Cucumber Raita (recipe follows)
4 slices tomato
4 whole wheat hamburger buns

1. Combine sirloin, turkey, lemon peel, oil, oregano, salt and pepper; mix well and shape into 8 patties. Make small depression in each of 4 patties and place ¼ of the cheese in each depression. Cover each with remaining 4 patties, sealing edges to form burgers.

2. Grill burgers 10 to 12 minutes or until thoroughly cooked, turning once. Serve with Cucumber Raita and tomato slice on whole wheat bun. *Makes 4 burgers*

Cucumber Raita

1 cup plain nonfat yogurt
½ cup finely chopped cucumber
1 tablespoon minced fresh mint leaves
1 clove garlic, minced
¼ teaspoon salt

1. Combine all ingredients in small bowl. Cover and refrigerate until ready to use.

In medium bowl, combine all ingredients. Form into 4-inch patties. Broil or grill 4 to 6 minutes on each side or until cooked through. Serve immediately. *Makes 5 servings*

Cajun Chicken Burgers

1 pound fresh ground chicken or turkey
1 small onion, finely chopped
¼ cup chopped bell pepper
3 scallions, minced
1 clove garlic, minced
1 teaspoon **Worcestershire** sauce
½ teaspoon **TABASCO®** brand Pepper Sauce
Dash ground pepper

Grilled Feta Burger

Hawaiian-Style Burgers

1 ½ pounds ground beef
⅓ cup chopped green onions
2 tablespoons Worcestershire sauce
⅛ teaspoon pepper
⅓ cup pineapple preserves
⅓ cup barbecue sauce
6 pineapple slices
6 hamburger buns, split and toasted

1. Combine beef, onions, Worcestershire and pepper in large bowl. Shape into six 1-inch-thick patties.

2. Combine preserves and barbecue sauce in small saucepan. Bring to a boil over medium heat, stirring often.

3. Place patties on grill rack directly above medium coals. Grill, uncovered, until desired doneness, turning and brushing often with sauce. Place pineapple on grill; grill 1 minute or until browned, turning once.

4. To serve, place patties on buns with pineapple.

Makes 6 servings

Broiling Directions: Arrange patties on rack in broiler pan. Broil 4 inches from heat until desired doneness, turning and brushing often with sauce. Broil pineapple 1 minute, turning once.

Grilled Salmon Burgers

1 pound fresh boneless, skinless salmon
2 tablespoons sliced green onions
1 teaspoon LAWRY'S® Garlic Pepper
½ teaspoon LAWRY'S® Seasoned Salt
2 tablespoons LAWRY'S® Citrus Grill Marinade with Orange Juice

Add all ingredients to food processor. Process on pulse setting until salmon is well minced. Place mixture in medium bowl; mix well. Form into 4 patties. Broil or grill, 4 to 5 inches from heat source, 3 to 4 minutes on each side, or until cooked through.

Makes 4 servings

Serving Suggestion: Serve on warm toasted hamburger buns.

Hawaiian-Style Burger

Inside-Out Brie Burgers

1 pound ground beef
**5 tablespoons A.1.® Original
   or A.1.® Bold & Spicy
   Steak Sauce, divided**
3 ounces Brie, cut into 4 slices
¼ cup dairy sour cream
**2 tablespoons chopped green
   onion**
**1 medium-size red bell
   pepper, cut into 1/4-inch
   rings**
**4 (2½-inch) slices Italian or
   French bread, halved**
4 radicchio or lettuce leaves

In medium bowl, combine beef and 3 tablespoons steak sauce; shape into 8 thin patties. Place 1 slice Brie in center of each of 4 patties. Top with remaining patties. Seal edges to form 4 patties; set aside.

In small bowl, combine sour cream, remaining 2 tablespoons steak sauce and green onion; set aside.

Grill burgers over medium heat or broil 6 inches from heat source 7 minutes on each side or until beef is no longer pink. Place pepper rings on grill or under broiler; cook with burgers until tender, about 4 to 5 minutes. Top each of 4 bread slice halves with radicchio leaf, pepper ring, burger, 2 tablespoons reserved sauce and another bread slice half. Serve immediately. Garnish as desired.

Makes 4 servings

Western Onion Cheeseburgers

1 pound ground beef
**1⅓ cups FRENCH'S® French
   Fried Onions, divided**
**¼ cup finely chopped green
   bell pepper**
¼ cup barbecue sauce
½ teaspoon garlic powder
**¼ teaspoon ground black
   pepper**
4 thick slices Cheddar cheese
4 hamburger rolls

Combine beef, ⅔ cup French Fried Onions, bell pepper, barbecue sauce, garlic powder and ground pepper in large bowl. Shape into 4 patties.

Place patties on oiled grid. Grill* over medium coals 10 minutes or until no longer pink in center, turning once. Place 1 slice cheese on each burger. Cook until cheese melts. Serve on rolls. Top with remaining ⅔ cup onions.

Makes 4 servings

*Or, broil 6 inches from heat.

Prep Time: *10 minutes*
Cook Time: *10 minutes*

Inside-Out Brie Burger

Mediterranean Burgers

½ cup feta cheese (2 ounces)
¼ cup A.1. Original or A.1.
　　Bold & Spicy Steak Sauce,
　　divided
2 tablespoons sliced pitted
　　ripe olives
2 tablespoons mayonnaise
1 pound ground beef
4 (5-inch) pita breads
4 radicchio leaves
4 tomato slices

In small bowl, combine feta cheese, 2 tablespoons steak sauce, olives and mayonnaise. Cover; refrigerate at least 1 hour or up to 2 days.

Shape beef into 4 patties. Grill burgers over medium heat or broil 6 inches from heat source 5 minutes on each side or until no longer pink in center, basting with remaining 2 tablespoons steak sauce. Split open top edge of each pita bread. Arrange 1 radicchio leaf in each pita pocket; top each with burger, tomato slice and 2 tablespoons chilled sauce. Serve immediately.   *Makes 4 servings*

Backyard Barbecue Turkey Burgers

2 packages (1¼ pounds each)
　　BUTTERBALL® Lean
　　Fresh Ground Turkey
1 cup chopped onion
1 cup prepared barbecue
　　sauce, divided
1 cup dry bread crumbs
1 teaspoon salt
¼ teaspoon black pepper
12 hamburger buns, toasted

Combine ground turkey, onion, ½ cup barbecue sauce, bread crumbs, salt and pepper in large bowl. Mix until thoroughly combined. Form into 12 patties. Grill over hot coals 5 to 6 minutes on each side or cook in large nonstick skillet over medium heat 10 to 12 minutes or until no longer pink in center. Turn 2 to 3 times for even browning. Serve on buns with remaining ½ cup barbecue sauce on the side.

Makes 12 burgers

Preparation Time: *15 minutes*

Mediterranean Burger

Mexicali Burgers

        Guacamole (recipe follows)
    1 pound ground beef
    ⅓ cup prepared salsa or
        picante sauce
    ⅓ cup crushed tortilla chips
    3 tablespoons finely chopped
        cilantro
    2 tablespoons finely chopped
        onion
    1 teaspoon ground cumin
    4 slices Monterey Jack or
        Cheddar cheese
    4 Kaiser rolls or hamburger
        buns, split
        Lettuce leaves (optional)
        Sliced tomatoes (optional)

To prevent sticking, spray grill with nonstick cooking spray. Prepare coals for grilling. Meanwhile, prepare Guacamole.

Combine beef, salsa, tortilla chips, cilantro, onion and cumin in medium bowl until well blended. Shape mixture into 4 burgers. Place burgers on grill, 6 inches from medium coals. Grill, covered, 8 to 10 minutes for medium or until desired doneness is reached, turning once. Place 1 slice cheese on each burger during last 1 to 2 minutes of grilling. If desired, place rolls, cut-side down, on grill to toast lightly during last 1 to 2 minutes of grilling. Place burgers between rolls; top burgers with Guacamole. Serve with lettuce and tomatoes. Garnish as desired. *Makes 4 servings*

Guacamole

    1 ripe avocado, seeded
    1 tablespoon salsa or picante sauce
    1 teaspoon lime or lemon juice
    ¼ teaspoon garlic salt

Place avocado in medium bowl; mash with fork until avocado is slightly chunky. Add salsa, lime juice and garlic salt; blend well.
Makes about ½ cup

Mexicali Burger

Mushroom-Stuffed Pork Burgers

¾ **cup thinly sliced fresh
    mushrooms**
¼ **cup thinly sliced green onion**
1 **clove garlic, minced**
2 **teaspoons butter or
    margarine**
1 ½ **pounds lean ground pork**
1 **teaspoon Dijon-style
    mustard**
1 **teaspoon Worcestershire
    sauce**
¼ **teaspoon salt**
⅛ **teaspoon freshly ground
    pepper**

In skillet, sauté mushrooms, onion and garlic in butter until tender, about 2 minutes; set aside.

Combine ground pork, mustard, Worcestershire sauce, salt and pepper; mix well. Shape into 12 patties, about 4 inches in diameter. Spoon mushroom mixture onto center of 6 patties. Spread to within ½ inch of edges. Top with remaining 6 patties; seal edges.

Place patties on grill about 6 inches over medium coals. Grill 10 to 15 minutes or until cooked through, turning once. Serve on buns, if desired.
Makes 6 servings

Prep Time: *15 minutes*
Cook Time: *15 minutes*

Favorite recipe from **National Pork Producers Council**

Black Gold Burgers

¾ **cup finely chopped onion**
6 **large cloves garlic, minced
    (about 3 tablespoons)**
2 **tablespoons margarine**
1 **tablespoon sugar**
¾ **cup A.1.® Original or A.1.®
    Bold & Spicy Steak Sauce**
1 ½ **pounds ground beef**
6 **onion rolls, split**

In medium skillet, over medium heat, cook and stir onion and garlic in margarine until tender but not brown; stir in sugar. Reduce heat to low; cook for 10 minutes. Stir in steak sauce; keep warm. Shape ground beef into 6 patties. Grill burgers over medium heat for 5 minutes on each side or until done. Place burgers on roll bottoms; top each with 3 tablespoons sauce and roll top. Serve immediately; garnish as desired.
Makes 6 servings

Mushroom-Stuffed Pork Burger

Polynesian Burgers

¼ cup **LAWRY'S**® Teriyaki
   Marinade with Pineapple
   Juice
1 pound ground beef
½ cup chopped green bell
   pepper
4 onion-flavored hamburger
   buns
1 can (5¼ ounces) pineapple
   slices, drained
   Lettuce leaves

In medium bowl, combine Teriyaki Marinade, ground beef and bell pepper; mix well. Let stand 10 to 15 minutes. Shape into 4 patties. Grill or broil burgers 8 to 10 minutes or until desired doneness, turning halfway through grilling time. Serve burgers on onion buns topped with pineapple slices and lettuce.   *Makes 4 servings*

Serving Suggestion: Serve with assorted fresh fruits.

Hint: For extra teriyaki flavor, brush buns and pineapple slices with additional Teriyaki Marinade; grill or broil until buns are lightly toasted and pineapple is heated through.

Pizza Burgers

1 pound lean ground beef
1 cup (4 ounces) shredded
   mozzarella cheese
1 tablespoon minced onion
1½ teaspoons chopped fresh
   oregano *or* ½ teaspoon
   dried oregano leaves
1 tablespoon chopped fresh
   basil *or* 1 teaspoon dried
   basil leaves
½ teaspoon salt
   Dash freshly ground pepper
   Prepared pizza sauce,
   heated
   English muffins

Preheat grill.

Combine ground beef, cheese, onion, oregano, basil, salt and pepper in medium bowl; mix lightly. Shape into four patties.

Grill 8 minutes or to desired doneness, turning once. Top with pizza sauce. Serve on English muffins.   *Makes 4 servings*

Polynesian Burger

Ranch Burgers

1¼ pounds lean ground beef
¾ cup prepared **HIDDEN VALLEY® Original Ranch® Salad Dressing**
¾ cup dry bread crumbs
¼ cup minced onions
1 teaspoon salt
¼ teaspoon black pepper
  Sesame seed buns
  Lettuce, tomato slices and red onion slices (optional)
  Additional Original Ranch® Salad Dressing

In large bowl, combine beef, salad dressing, bread crumbs, onions, salt and pepper. Shape into 6 patties. Grill over medium-hot coals 4 to 5 minutes for medium doneness. Place on sesame seed buns with lettuce, tomato and red onion slices, if desired. Serve with a generous amount of additional salad dressing.   *Makes 6 servings*

Stuffed Cheese Burgers

1½ cups shredded Monterey Jack cheese (about 6 ounces)
1 can (2¼ ounces) chopped black olives, drained
⅛ teaspoon hot pepper sauce
1¾ pounds ground beef
¼ cup finely chopped onion
1 teaspoon salt
½ teaspoon black pepper
6 whole wheat hamburger buns
  Butter or margarine, melted

Combine cheese, olives and hot pepper sauce; mix well. Divide mixture evenly and shape into 6 balls. Mix ground beef with onion, salt and pepper; shape into 12 thin patties. Place a cheese ball in center of 6 patties and top each with a second patty. Seal edges of each patty to enclose cheese ball. Lightly oil grid. Grill patties, on covered grill, over medium-hot KINGSFORD® Briquets 5 to 6 minutes on each side or until done.

Split buns, brush with butter and place cut-sides down on grill to heat through. Serve on buns.   *Makes 6 servings*

Ranch Burger

Vegetarian Burgers

½ cup A.1.® Steak Sauce,
  divided
¼ cup plain yogurt
⅔ cup PLANTERS® Slivered
  Almonds
⅔ cup PLANTERS® Cocktail
  Peanuts
⅔ cup PLANTERS® Sunflower
  Kernels
½ cup chopped green bell
  pepper
¼ cup chopped onion
1 clove garlic, minced
1 tablespoon red wine vinegar
4 (5-inch) pita breads, halved
4 lettuce leaves
4 tomato slices

In small bowl, combine ¼ cup steak sauce and yogurt; set aside. In food processor or blender, process almonds, peanuts, sunflower kernels, green pepper, onion and garlic until coarsely chopped. With motor running, slowly add remaining Steak Sauce and vinegar until blended; shape mixture into 4 patties. Grill burgers over medium heat for 1½ minutes on each side or until heated through, turning once. Split open top edge of each pita bread. Layer lettuce, burger, tomato slice and 2 tablespoons prepared sauce in each pita bread half. Serve immediately.

Makes 4 servings

Fiery Boursin Burgers

1 pound lean ground beef
1 egg, beaten
1 tablespoon Worcestershire
  Sauce
¾ teaspoon TABASCO® brand
  Pepper Sauce
1 package (5 ounces) boursin
  or herbed chèvre cheese

Preheat broiler or prepare grill.

In medium bowl, combine beef, egg, Worcestershire and TABASCO® Sauce until well mixed. Divide into five portions.

Form three-quarters of each portion into a patty, reserving the remainder. Make indentation in center of each patty and fill with 2 tablespoons of the cheese. Cover cheese with reserved meat and form a finished patty.

Broil or grill patties 3 to 5 minutes on each side or to desired doneness. Serve immediately.

Makes 5 servings

Vegetarian Burger

Tasty Taco Burgers

1 pound ground beef
1 package (1¼ ounces) taco
   seasoning mix
8 KRAFT® American Singles
   Pasteurized Process
   Cheese Food
4 Kaiser rolls, split
   Lettuce leaves
   Salsa
   BREAKSTONE'S® or
   KNUDSEN® Sour Cream
   (optional)

MIX 1 pound ground beef and taco seasoning mix. Shape into 4 patties.

GRILL patties over hot coals 6 to 8 minutes on each side or to desired doneness. Top each patty with 2 process cheese food slices. Continue grilling until process cheese food is melted.

FILL rolls with lettuce and cheeseburgers. Top with salsa and sour cream, if desired.

Makes 4 servings

Teriyaki Burgers

1 pound ground beef
6 tablespoons A.1.® Steak
   Sauce, divided
¼ cup finely chopped water
   chestnuts
3 tablespoons teriyaki sauce
1 clove garlic, minced
1 (8-ounce) can pineapple
   slices, drained
4 hamburger rolls, split
4 lettuce leaves
4 red onion slices

In medium bowl, combine ground beef, 3 tablespoons steak sauce and water chestnuts; shape mixture into 4 patties. Set aside.

In small bowl, combine remaining steak sauce, teriyaki sauce and garlic; set aside.

Grill pineapple slices over medium heat for 1 minute on each side or until heated through; keep warm. Grill burgers over medium heat for 5 minutes on each side or until done, brushing often with teriyaki mixture. Top each roll bottom with lettuce leaf, burger, onion slice, pineapple slice and roll top; serve immediately.

Makes 4 servings

Tasty Taco Burger

Ranchero Onion Burgers

1 pound ground beef
½ cup salsa
½ cup (2 ounces) shredded Monterey Jack cheese
1⅓ cups FRENCH'S® French Fried Onions, divided
½ teaspoon garlic powder
¼ teaspoon ground black pepper
4 hamburger rolls

Scandinavian Burgers

1 pound lean ground beef
¾ cup shredded zucchini
⅓ cup shredded carrots
2 tablespoons finely minced onion
1 tablespoon fresh chopped dill *or* 1 teaspoon dried dill weed
½ teaspoon salt
Dash freshly ground pepper
1 egg, beaten
¼ cup beer

Combine beef, salsa, cheese, ⅔ *cup* French Fried Onions, garlic powder and pepper in large bowl. Shape into 4 patties.

Place patties on oiled grid. Grill* over medium coals 10 minutes or until no longer pink in center, turning once. Serve on rolls. Garnish with additional salsa, if desired. Top with remaining ⅔ *cup* onions.

Makes 4 servings

*Or, broil 6 inches from heat.

Tip: For extra-crispy warm onion flavor, heat French Fried Onions in the microwave for 1 minute. Or, place in foil pan and heat on the grill 2 minutes.

Prep Time: *10 minutes*
Cook Time: *10 minutes*

Preheat grill.

Combine ground beef, zucchini, carrots, onion, dill, salt and pepper in medium bowl; mix lightly. Stir in egg and beer. Shape into 4 patties.

Grill 8 minutes or to desired doneness, turning once. Serve on whole wheat buns or rye rolls, if desired. *Makes 4 servings*

Ranchero Onion Burger

Basil Chicken and Vegetables on Focaccia

½ cup mayonnaise
¼ teaspoon garlic powder
½ teaspoon black pepper,
    divided
1 loaf (16 ounces) focaccia or
    Italian bread, sliced
4 boneless skinless chicken
    breast halves (about
    1¼ pounds)
3 tablespoons olive oil
2 cloves garlic, minced
1½ teaspoons dried basil leaves
½ teaspoon salt
1 green bell pepper, stemmed,
    seeded and cut into
    quarters
1 medium zucchini, cut
    lengthwise into 4 slices
2 Italian plum tomatoes,
    sliced

Combine mayonnaise, garlic powder and ¼ teaspoon black pepper in small bowl; set aside.

Cut focaccia into quarters. Cut each quarter horizontally in half; set aside.

Combine chicken, oil, garlic, basil, salt and remaining ¼ teaspoon black pepper in large resealable plastic food storage bag. Seal bag; knead to combine. Add bell pepper and zucchini; knead to coat.

Grill or broil chicken, bell pepper and zucchini 4 inches from heat source 6 to 8 minutes on each side or until chicken is no longer pink in center. (Bell pepper and zucchini may take less time.)

Top bottom half of each focaccia quarter with tomatoes, bell pepper, zucchini and chicken. Spread bread with mayonnaise. Top with focaccia tops. *Makes 6 servings*

Basil Chicken and Vegetables on Focaccia

Grilled Steak 'n' Vegetable-Topped Pizzas

1 (1-pound) beef top round steak, thinly sliced and cut into julienne strips
3 tablespoons olive oil, divided
¾ cup purchased or homemade spaghetti sauce
½ cup A.1.® Original or A.1.® Bold & Spicy Steak Sauce
1 pound frozen bread or pizza dough, thawed
2 cups shredded mozzarella cheese (8 ounces)
¼ cup chopped fresh tomato
¼ cup sliced green onions
¼ cup sliced pitted ripe olives

In medium skillet, over medium-high heat, sauté steak strips in 1 tablespoon oil until no longer pink; drain. Stir in spaghetti and steak sauces; cook and stir until heated through. Keep warm.

Divide dough in half; shape each piece into 8-inch round. Brush one side of each dough round with ½ tablespoon oil. Grill pizza rounds, oil sides down, over low heat 5 to 7 minutes or until dough is firm and brown. Brush tops of dough with remaining 1 tablespoon oil; turn over dough rounds. Top dough rounds evenly with warm meat mixture, cheese, tomato, green onions and olives. Grill, covered with lid or foil, 5 to 7 minutes more or until bottom is golden and cheese melts. Cut into wedges. Serve immediately.

Makes 2 (8-inch) pizza rounds

Hot Off The Grill

For barbecue safety, position the grill on a heat-proof surface, away from trees and bushes that could catch a spark and out of the path of traffic. Also, make sure the grill's vents are not clogged with ashes before starting a fire.

Grilled Steak 'n' Vegetable-Topped Pizzas

Barbecued Pork Tenderloin Sandwiches

½ cup ketchup
⅓ cup packed brown sugar
2 tablespoons bourbon or
    whiskey (optional)
1 tablespoon Worcestershire
    sauce
½ teaspoon dry mustard
¼ teaspoon ground red pepper
1 clove garlic, minced
2 whole pork tenderloins
    (about ¾ pound each),
    well trimmed
1 large red onion, cut into 6
    (¼-inch-thick) slices
6 hoagie rolls or Kaiser rolls,
    split

1. Prepare barbecue grill for direct cooking.

2. Combine ketchup, sugar, bourbon, Worcestershire sauce, mustard, ground red pepper and garlic in small, heavy saucepan with ovenproof handle; mix well.

3. Set saucepan on one side of grid.* Place tenderloins on center of grid. Grill tenderloins, on uncovered grill, over medium-hot coals 8 minutes. Simmer sauce 5 minutes or until thickened, stirring occasionally.

4. Turn tenderloins with tongs; continue to grill, uncovered, 5 minutes. Add onion slices to grid. Set aside half of sauce; reserve. Brush tenderloins and onion with a portion of remaining sauce.

5. Continue to grill, uncovered, 7 to 10 minutes or until pork is juicy and barely pink in center, brushing with remaining sauce and turning onion and tenderloins halfway through grilling time. (If desired, insert instant-read thermometer** into center of thickest part of tenderloins. Thermometer should register 160°F.)

6. Carve tenderloins crosswise into thin slices; separate onion slices into rings. Divide meat and onion rings among rolls; drizzle with reserved sauce. *Makes 6 servings*

*If desired, sauce may be prepared on range-top. Combine ketchup, sugar, bourbon, Worcestershire sauce, mustard, ground red pepper and garlic in small saucepan. Bring to a boil over medium-high heat. Reduce heat to low and simmer, uncovered, 5 minutes or until thickened, stirring occasionally.

**Do not leave instant-read thermometer in tenderloins during grilling since the thermometer is not heatproof.

Barbecued Pork Tenderloin Sandwich

Caramelized Onion & Eggplant Sandwiches

**Grilled Garlic Aioli (recipe
follows) or mayonnaise**
½ cup packed brown sugar
½ cup water
½ cup soy sauce
2 tablespoons molasses
5 slices fresh ginger
¼ teaspoon ground coriander
Dash black pepper
1 large yellow onion
**4 large eggplant slices, 1 inch
thick**
4 round buns, split
4 tomato slices
Mixed greens
Radishes
Carrot curls

Prepare Grilled Garlic Aioli; set aside. Combine sugar, water, soy sauce, molasses, ginger, coriander and pepper in small saucepan. Bring to boil, stirring constantly. Reduce heat; simmer marinade 5 minutes, stirring occasionally. Cool. Cut onion into ½-inch-thick slices. Insert wooden picks into onion slices from edges to prevent separating into rings. (Soak wooden picks in hot water 15 minutes to prevent burning.) Marinate eggplant and onion in marinade 10 to 15 minutes. Remove vegetables from marinade; reserve marinade. Lightly oil grid to prevent sticking. Grill vegetables on covered grill around edge of medium-hot KINGSFORD® Briquets about 20 minutes or until tender, turning once or twice and brushing with reserved marinade. Place buns on grill, cut sides down, until toasted. Serve eggplant and onion on grilled buns with tomato, greens and Grilled Garlic Aioli. Garnish with radishes and carrot curls. *Makes 4 sandwiches*

Grilled Garlic Aioli: Prepare Grilled Garlic (recipe follows). Mash 8 cloves Grilled Garlic in small bowl. Add ¼ cup mayonnaise; mix until blended.

Grilled Garlic: Peel outermost papery skin from 1 or 2 garlic heads. Brush garlic with olive oil. Grill at edge of grid on covered grill over medium-hot KINGSFORD® Briquets 30 to 45 minutes or until cloves are soft and buttery. Remove from grill; cool slightly. Gently squeeze softened garlic head from root end so that cloves slip out of skins into small bowl. Use immediately or cover and refrigerate up to 1 week.

Caramelized Onion & Eggplant Sandwich

Grilled Chile Chicken Quesadillas

2 tablespoons lime juice
3 cloves garlic, minced
1 tablespoon ground cumin
1 tablespoon chili powder
1 tablespoon vegetable oil
1 jalapeño pepper, minced
1 teaspoon salt
6 boneless skinless chicken
   thighs
3 poblano peppers, cut in half,
   stemmed, seeded
2 avocados, peeled and sliced
3 cups (12 ounces) shredded
   Monterey Jack cheese
12 (8-inch) flour tortillas
1½ cups fresh salsa
   Red chiles
   Fresh cilantro sprigs

Combine lime juice, garlic, cumin, chili powder, oil, jalapeño pepper and salt in small bowl; coat chicken with paste. Cover and refrigerate chicken at least 15 minutes. Grill chicken on covered grill over medium-hot KINGSFORD® Briquets 4 minutes per side until no longer pink in center. Grill poblano peppers, skin side down, 8 minutes until skins are charred. Place peppers in large resealable plastic food storage bag; seal. Let stand 5 minutes; remove skin. Cut chicken and peppers into strips. Arrange chicken, peppers, avocado and cheese on half of each tortilla. Drizzle with 2 tablespoons salsa. Fold other half of tortilla over filling. Grill quesadillas on covered grill over medium briquets 30 seconds to 1 minute per side until cheese is melted. Garnish with chiles and cilantro sprigs. *Makes 12 quesadillas*

Hot Off The Grill

Use long-handled tongs or a spatula to turn meat. A fork or knife punctures meat and lets the juices escape.

Grilled Chile Chicken Quesadillas

Chicago Fire Italian Sausage Sandwiches

1 package BUTTERBALL®
Lean Fresh Turkey Hot
Italian Sausage
5 large hot dog buns
5 teaspoons yellow mustard
5 tablespoons chopped onion
5 tablespoons pickle relish
10 tomato wedges
10 hot sport peppers

Grill sausage according to package directions. Place in buns. Add mustard, onion, relish, tomato wedges and peppers to each sandwich.

Makes 5 sandwiches

Preparation Time: *15 minutes*

Grilled Chicken Sandwiches Monterey

⅓ cup dairy sour cream*
⅓ cup prepared chunky salsa
¼ cup GREY POUPON® Dijon
Mustard, divided
4 boneless, skinless chicken
breasts, pounded slightly
(about 1 pound)
8 slices Muenster cheese
(4 ounces)
4 croissants
1 cup shredded lettuce
8 slices tomato
4 slices ripe avocado

Lowfat sour cream may be substituted for regular sour cream.

In small bowl, blend sour cream, salsa and 2 tablespoons mustard; set sauce aside.

Grill or broil chicken for 8 to 10 minutes or until done, turning and brushing with remaining mustard. Top each breast with 2 slices cheese; cook 1 minute more or until cheese melts.

Cut croissants in half; spread cut sides with ¼ cup prepared sauce. Place ¼ cup lettuce on each croissant bottom; top with chicken breast, 2 tomato slices, 1 avocado slice and croissant top. Serve with remaining sauce.

Makes 4 sandwiches

Chicago Fire Italian Sausage Sandwich

Grilled Chicken Breast and Peperonata Sandwiches

1 tablespoon olive oil or
    vegetable oil
1 medium red bell pepper,
    sliced into strips
1 medium green bell pepper,
    sliced into strips
¾ cup onion slices (about
    1 medium)
2 cloves garlic, minced
¼ teaspoon salt
¼ teaspoon black pepper
4 boneless skinless chicken
    breast halves (about
    1 pound)
4 small French rolls, split and
    toasted

1. Heat oil in large nonstick skillet over medium heat until hot. Add bell peppers, onion and garlic; cook and stir 5 minutes. Reduce heat to low; cook and stir about 20 minutes or until vegetables are very soft. Sprinkle with salt and black pepper.

2. Grill chicken, on covered grill over medium-hot coals, 10 minutes on each side or until chicken is no longer pink in center. Or, broil chicken, 6 inches from heat source, 7 to 8 minutes on each side or until chicken is no longer pink in center.

3. Place chicken in rolls. Divide pepper mixture evenly; spoon over chicken.

Makes 4 servings

Hot Off The Grill

To get a sluggish fire going, place two to three additional coals in a small metal can and add lighter fluid. Then stack them on the coals in the grill and light with a match.

Grilled Chicken Breast and Peperonata Sandwich

Pesto Chicken & Pepper Wraps

⅔ cup refrigerated pesto sauce or frozen pesto sauce, thawed and divided
3 tablespoons red wine vinegar
¼ teaspoon salt
¼ teaspoon black pepper
1¼ pounds skinless boneless chicken thighs or breasts
2 red bell peppers, cut in half, stemmed and seeded
5 (8-inch) flour tortillas
5 thin slices (3-inch rounds) fresh-pack mozzarella cheese*
5 leaves Boston or red leaf lettuce
Orange slices
Red and green chilies
Fresh basil sprigs

Packaged sliced whole milk or part-skim mozzarella cheese can be substituted for fresh-pack mozzarella cheese.

Combine ¼ cup pesto, vinegar, salt and black pepper in medium bowl. Add chicken; toss to coat. Cover and refrigerate at least 30 minutes. Remove chicken from marinade; discard marinade. Grill chicken over medium-hot KINGSFORD® Briquets about 4 minutes per side until chicken is no longer pink in center, turning once. Grill bell peppers, skin sides down, about 8 minutes until skin is charred. Place bell peppers in large resealable plastic food storage bag; seal. Let stand 5 minutes; remove skin. Cut chicken and bell peppers into thin strips. Spread about 1 tablespoon of remaining pesto down center of each tortilla; top with chicken, bell peppers, cheese and lettuce. Roll tortillas to enclose filling. Garnish with orange slices, chilies and basil sprigs.

Makes 5 wraps

Hot Off The Grill

Toss a little prepared pesto into deli potato salad for a wonderful addition to this fabulous sandwich. Voila, your meal is complete.

Pesto Chicken & Pepper Wrap

Grilled Chicken Croissant with Roasted Pepper Dressing

½ cup **FRENCH'S® Dijon Mustard**
3 tablespoons olive oil
3 tablespoons red wine vinegar
¾ teaspoon dried Italian seasoning
¾ teaspoon garlic powder
1 jar (7 ounces) roasted red peppers, drained
1 pound boneless skinless chicken breast halves
Lettuce leaves
4 croissants, split

Whisk together mustard, oil, vinegar and seasonings in small bowl until well blended. Pour ¼ cup mixture into blender. Add peppers. Cover and process until mixture is smooth; set aside.

Brush chicken pieces with remaining mustard mixture. Place pieces on grid. Grill over hot coals 15 minutes or until chicken is no longer pink in center, turning often. To serve, place lettuce leaves on bottom halves of croissants. Arrange chicken on top of lettuce. Spoon roasted pepper dressing over chicken. Cover with croissant top. Garnish as desired. *Makes 4 servings*

Prep Time: *15 minutes*
Cook Time: *15 minutes*

Hot Off The Grill

To check the temperature of the coals, cautiously hold the palm of your hand at grid level—over the coals for direct heat—and count the number of seconds you can hold your hand in that position before the heat forces you to pull away. For a hot grill (about 375°F or more), you should be able to hold your hand there for 2 seconds.

Grilled Chicken Croissant with Roasted Pepper Dressing

Grilled Vegetable & Cheese Sandwiches

**2 large zucchini squash, cut
    lengthwise into eight
    ¼-inch slices**
**4 slices sweet onion (such as
    Vidalia or Walla Walla)
    cut ¼ inch thick**
**1 large yellow bell pepper, cut
    lengthwise into quarters**
**6 tablespoons prepared light
    or regular Caesar salad
    dressing, divided**
8 oval slices sourdough bread
**6 (1-ounce) slices Muenster
    cheese**

1. Prepare barbecue for grilling. Brush both sides of vegetables with ¼ cup dressing. Place vegetables on grid over medium coals. Grill on covered grill 5 minutes. Turn; grill 2 minutes.

2. Brush both sides of bread lightly with remaining 2 tablespoons dressing. Place bread around vegetables; grill 2 minutes or until bread is lightly toasted. Turn bread; top 4 pieces of bread with 4 slices of cheese. Tear remaining 2 cheese slices into small pieces; place on bread around cheese. Grill vegetables and bread 1 to 2 minutes more or until cheese is melted, bread is toasted and vegetables are crisp-tender.

3. Arrange vegetables over cheese side of bread; top with remaining bread. *Makes 4 servings*

Serving Suggestion: Serve with a fresh fruit salad.

Prep and Cook Time: *22 minutes*

Chicken Teriyaki Wraps

**1½ cups LAWRY'S® Teriyaki
    Marinade with Pineapple
    Juice, divided**
**6 boneless, skinless chicken
    breast halves (about
    1½ pounds)**
½ pound bean sprouts
**3½ cups shredded bok choy or
    lettuce**
**1 can (8 ounces) sliced water
    chestnuts, drained**
12 flour tortillas, warmed

In large resealable plastic food storage bag, combine 1 cup Teriyaki Marinade and chicken; seal bag. Marinate in refrigerator at least 30 minutes. Remove chicken; discard used marinade. Grill or broil chicken 10 to 15 minutes or until no longer pink in center and juices run clear when cut, turning halfway through grilling time. Cut chicken into thin strips. Refrigerate 30 minutes or until chilled. In large bowl, place chicken, bean sprouts, bok choy, water chestnuts and additional ¼ cup Teriyaki Marinade. Toss until well coated. Spread additional Teriyaki Marinade on each tortilla; top each with ¾ cup chicken mixture. Wrap to enclose filling. Serve immediately. *Makes 6 servings*

Serving Suggestion: Serve with fresh melon wedges or mango slices.

Grilled Vegetable & Cheese Sandwiches

Magic Carpet Kabobs

1 cup orange juice
½ cup bottled mango chutney, divided
2 tablespoons lemon juice
1 tablespoon grated fresh ginger
2 cloves garlic, pressed
2 teaspoons ground cumin
1 teaspoon grated lemon peel
1 teaspoon grated orange peel
1 teaspoon red pepper flakes
¼ teaspoon salt
4 boneless skinless chicken thighs, cut into chunks
1 medium yellow onion, cut into chunks
4 whole pita bread rounds
½ cup plain low-fat yogurt
¾ cup chopped cucumber
Orange peel strips

Combine orange juice, ¼ cup chutney, lemon juice, ginger, garlic, cumin, grated peels, pepper and salt, blending well; reserve ¼ cup marinade for basting. Combine remaining marinade and chicken in large resealable plastic food storage bag. Seal bag; turn to coat evenly. Marinate in refrigerator overnight. Thread chicken alternately with onion onto 4 long wooden skewers, dividing equally. (Soak wooden skewers in hot water 30 minutes to prevent burning.) Lightly oil grid to prevent sticking. Grill kabobs over medium-hot KINGSFORD® Briquets 10 to 12 minutes until chicken is no longer pink, turning once and basting with reserved marinade. Grill pita breads 1 or 2 minutes until warm. Combine yogurt and remaining ¼ cup chutney. Spoon yogurt mixture down centers of pitas; top with cucumber, dividing equally. Top each with kabob; remove skewer. Garnish with orange peel strips.

Makes 4 servings

Hot Off The Grill

In hot weather, food should never sit out for more than 1 hour. Remember, keep hot foods hot and cold foods cold to avoid food contamination.

Magic Carpet Kabobs

Grilled Chicken & Fresh Salsa Wraps

1¼ cups **LAWRY'S®** Herb &
    Garlic Marinade with
    Lemon Juice, divided
4 boneless, skinless chicken
    breast halves (about
    1 pound)
1 large tomato, chopped
1 can (4 ounces) diced mild
    green chiles, drained
    (optional)
¼ cup thinly sliced green
    onions
1 tablespoon red wine vinegar
1 tablespoon chopped fresh
    cilantro
½ teaspoon **LAWRY'S®** Garlic
    Salt
4 to 8 flour tortillas, warmed

In large resealable plastic food storage bag, combine 1 cup Herb & Garlic Marinade and chicken; seal bag. Marinate in refrigerator at least 30 minutes. In medium bowl, combine tomato, chiles, if desired, green onions, additional ¼ cup Herb & Garlic Marinade, vinegar, cilantro and Garlic Salt; mix well. Cover and refrigerate 30 minutes or until chilled. Remove chicken; discard used marinade. Grill or broil chicken 10 to 15 minutes or until no longer pink in center and juices run clear when cut, turning halfway through grilling time. Cut chicken into strips. Place chicken on tortillas; spoon salsa on top and wrap to enclose. Serve immediately.

Makes 4 servings

Serving Suggestion: Serve with black bean and corn salad.

Hint: This is an excellent recipe for picnics or outdoor dining. Assemble wraps when ready to serve.

Hot Off The Grill

Watch food carefully during grilling. Total cooking time will vary with type of food, position on the grill, weather, temperature of the coals and degree of doneness you desire.

Grilled Chicken & Fresh Salsa Wrap

Maple Francheezies

Mustard Spread (recipe follows)
¼ cup maple syrup
2 teaspoons garlic powder
1 teaspoon black pepper
½ teaspoon ground nutmeg
4 slices bacon
4 jumbo hot dogs
4 hot dog buns, split
½ cup (2 ounces) shredded Cheddar cheese

Prepare Mustard Spread; set aside.

Prepare grill for direct cooking.

Combine maple syrup, garlic powder, pepper and nutmeg in small bowl. Brush syrup mixture onto bacon slices. Wrap 1 slice bacon around each hot dog.

Brush hot dogs with remaining syrup mixture. Place hot dogs on grid. Grill, covered, over medium-high heat 8 minutes or until bacon is crisp and hot dogs are heated through, turning halfway through grilling time. Place hot dogs in buns, top with Mustard Spread and cheese.   *Makes 4 servings*

Mustard Spread
½ cup prepared yellow mustard
1 tablespoon finely chopped onion
1 tablespoon diced tomato
1 tablespoon chopped fresh parsley
1 teaspoon garlic powder
½ teaspoon black pepper

Combine all ingredients in small bowl; mix well.

Makes about ¾ cup

Maple Francheezie

Maui Chicken Sandwich

1 can (8 ounces) **DOLE®**
   Pineapple Slices
½ teaspoon dried oregano
   leaves, crushed
¼ teaspoon garlic powder
4 skinless, boneless, small
   chicken breast halves
½ cup light prepared Thousand
   Island salad dressing
½ cup finely chopped jicama *or*
   water chestnuts
¼ teaspoon ground red pepper
   (optional)
4 whole grain or whole wheat
   sandwich rolls
   **DOLE® Red or Green Bell
   Pepper, sliced into rings or
   shredded DOLE® Iceberg
   Lettuce**

• Combine undrained pineapple, oregano and garlic powder in shallow, non-metallic dish. Add chicken; turn to coat all sides. Cover and marinate 15 minutes in refrigerator.

• Grill or broil chicken and pineapple, brushing occasionally with marinade, 5 to 8 minutes on each side or until chicken is no longer pink in center and pineapple is golden brown. Discard any remaining marinade.

• Combine dressing, jicama and red pepper. Spread on rolls. Top with chicken, pineapple and bell pepper rings. Serve open-face, if desired.   *Makes 4 servings*

Prep Time: *10 minutes*
Marinate Time: *15 minutes*
Cook Time: *15 minutes*

Maui Chicken Sandwich

Open-Faced Mesquite Steak Sandwiches

1 1/4 cups **LAWRY'S®** Mesquite
    Marinade with Lime Juice,
    divided
1 pound flank steak
8 slices sourdough or French
    bread
4 ounces refried beans
1 red onion, thinly sliced
1 green bell pepper, thinly
    sliced
1/2 cup chunky-style salsa
4 ounces cheddar cheese,
    thinly sliced

In large resealable plastic food storage bag, combine 3/4 cup Mesquite Marinade and steak; seal bag. Marinate in refrigerator at least 30 minutes. Remove steak; discard used marinade. Grill or broil steak 8 to 10 minutes or until desired doneness, turning once and basting often with additional 1/2 cup Mesquite Marinade. *Do not baste during last 5 minutes of cooking.* Discard any remaining marinade. Thinly slice steak on the diagonal across the grain. Spread bread slices with refried beans; top evenly with steak, onion and bell pepper. Top with salsa and cheese.

Makes 4 servings

Serving Suggestion: Serve warm with assorted crisp raw vegetables and iced tea.

Hint: Sandwich may be broiled to melt cheese, if desired.

Grilled Eggplant Sandwiches

1 eggplant (about 1 1/4
    pounds)
  Salt and black pepper
6 thin slices provolone cheese
6 thin slices deli-style ham or
    mortadella
  Fresh basil leaves (optional)
  Olive oil

Cut eggplant into 12 (3/8-inch-thick) rounds; sprinkle both sides with salt and pepper. Top each of 6 eggplant slices with slice of cheese, slice of meat (fold or tear to fit) and a few basil leaves, if desired. Cover with slice of eggplant. Brush one side with olive oil. Secure each sandwich with 2 or 3 toothpicks.

Oil hot grid to help prevent sticking. Grill eggplant, oil side down, on covered grill, over medium KINGSFORD® Briquets, 15 to 20 minutes. Halfway through cooking time, brush top with oil, then turn and continue grilling until eggplant is tender when pierced. (When turning, position sandwiches so toothpicks extend down between spaces in grid.) If eggplant starts to char, move to cooler part of grill. Let sandwiches cool about 5 minutes, then cut into halves or quarters, if desired. Serve warm or at room temperature.

Makes 6 sandwiches

Open-Faced Mesquite Steak Sandwiches

Moroccan Grilled Turkey with Cucumber Yogurt Sauce

**1 package BUTTERBALL®
Fresh Boneless Turkey
Breast Cutlets**
⅓ cup fresh lime juice
2 cloves garlic, minced
½ teaspoon curry powder
½ teaspoon salt
¼ teaspoon ground cumin
¼ teaspoon cayenne pepper
3 large pitas, cut in half*

Pitas may be filled and folded in half.

Prepare grill for medium-direct-heat cooking. Lightly spray unheated grill rack with nonstick cooking spray. Combine lime juice, garlic, curry powder, salt, cumin and cayenne pepper in medium bowl. Dip cutlets in lime juice mixture. Place cutlets on rack over medium-hot grill. Grill 5 to 7 minutes on each side or until meat is no longer pink in center. Place turkey and Cucumber Yogurt Sauce in pitas.

Serves 6

Cucumber Yogurt Sauce

1 cup fat free yogurt
½ cup shredded cucumber
1 teaspoon grated lime peel
1 teaspoon salt
½ teaspoon ground cumin

Combine yogurt, cucumber, lime peel, salt and cumin in medium bowl. Chill.

Preparation Time: *20 minutes*

Moroccan Grilled Turkey with Cucumber Yogurt Sauce

Grilled Vegetable Pizzas

1 package active dry quick-rise yeast
1 teaspoon sugar
⅔ cup warm water (105° to 115°F)
2 cups all-purpose flour
¾ teaspoon salt
3 tablespoons olive oil, divided
1 clove garlic, minced
1 red bell pepper, cut into quarters
4 slices red onion, cut ¼ inch thick
1 medium zucchini, halved lengthwise
1 medium yellow squash, halved lengthwise
1 cup purchased pizza sauce
¼ teaspoon crushed red pepper
2 cups (8 ounces) shredded fontinella or mozzarella cheese
¼ cup sliced fresh basil leaves

Sprinkle yeast and sugar over warm water in small bowl; stir until yeast is dissolved. Let stand 5 minutes or until mixture is bubbly. (If yeast does not bubble, it is no longer active. Discard mixture and start over with new yeast. Always check expiration date on yeast package. Also, water that is too hot will kill yeast; it is best to use a thermometer.) Combine flour, yeast mixture and salt in large bowl. Beat with electric mixer at medium speed until dough forms a ball. Add 1 tablespoon oil; beat until well mixed.

Place dough on lightly-floured surface; flatten slightly. Knead dough 8 to 9 minutes or until dough is smooth and elastic. Shape dough into a ball; place in large greased bowl. Turn to grease entire surface. Cover bowl with clean kitchen towel and let dough rise in warm place (80° to 85°F) 30 minutes or until doubled in bulk.

Meanwhile, prepare grill. Combine remaining 2 tablespoons oil and garlic in small bowl; brush over bell pepper, onion, zucchini and squash. Place vegetables on grid. Grill, on covered grill, over medium coals 10 minutes or until crisp-tender, turning halfway through grilling time. Remove vegetables. Slice pepper lengthwise into ¼-inch strips. Cut zucchini and squash crosswise into ¼-inch slices. Separate onion slices into rings.

Punch dough down; divide into 4 equal balls. Flatten each ball into circle on lightly floured surface. Using lightly floured rolling pin, roll out each ball, into 8-inch circle. Place 2 dough circles on grid. Grill, on covered grill, over medium coals 4 minutes or until bottoms are lightly browned. Transfer to large plates, grilled sides up. Repeat with remaining 2 dough circles.

Combine pizza sauce and crushed red pepper in small bowl; spread evenly over grilled sides of crusts. Sprinkle with cheese; top with grilled vegetables. Place 2 pizzas on grid. Grill, on covered grill, over medium coals 5 minutes or until cheese is melted and crusts are cooked through. Repeat with remaining 2 pizzas. Sprinkle pizzas with basil; cut into wedges. Serve warm or at room temperature.   *Makes 4 main-dish or 8 appetizer servings*

Grilled Vegetable Pizza

Vietnamese Grilled Steak Wraps

1 beef flank steak (about 1½ pounds)
Grated peel and juice of 2 lemons
6 tablespoons sugar, divided
2 tablespoons dark sesame oil
1¼ teaspoons salt, divided
½ teaspoon black pepper
¼ cup water
¼ cup rice vinegar
½ teaspoon crushed red pepper
6 (8-inch) flour tortillas
6 red leaf lettuce leaves
⅓ cup lightly packed fresh mint leaves
⅓ cup lightly packed fresh cilantro leaves
Star fruit slices
Red bell pepper strips
Orange peel strips

Cut beef across the grain into thin slices. Combine lemon peel, juice, 2 tablespoons sugar, sesame oil, 1 teaspoon salt and black pepper in medium bowl. Add beef; toss to coat. Cover and refrigerate at least 30 minutes. Combine water, vinegar, remaining 4 tablespoons sugar and ¼ teaspoon salt in small saucepan; bring to a boil. Boil 5 minutes without stirring until syrupy. Stir in crushed red pepper; set aside.

Remove beef from marinade; discard marinade. Thread beef onto metal or wooden skewers. (Soak wooden skewers in hot water 30 minutes to prevent burning.) Grill beef over medium-hot KINGSFORD® Briquets about 3 minutes per side until cooked through. Grill tortillas until hot. Place lettuce, beef, mint and cilantro on tortillas; drizzle with vinegar mixture. Roll tortillas to enclose filling. Garnish with star fruit, bell pepper and orange peel strips.

Makes 6 wraps

Hot Off The Grill

This recipe is excellent for picnics or outdoor dining. Simply assemble when you are ready to serve.

Vietnamese Grilled Steak Wrap

Patio-Perfect Beef & Lamb

Southwest Steak (page 160)

Lamb Chops with Fresh Herbs (page 190)

Beef Kabobs with Apricot Glaze

  1 can (15¼ ounces) **DEL MONTE®** Apricot
     Halves, undrained
  1 tablespoon cornstarch
  1 teaspoon Dijon mustard
 ½ teaspoon dried basil leaves
  1 pound sirloin steak, cut into 1½-inch cubes
  1 small green bell pepper, cut into ¾-inch pieces
  4 medium mushrooms, cut in half
  4 to 8 skewers*

*To prevent burning of wooden skewers, soak skewers in water for 10 minutes before assembling kabobs.

1. Drain apricot syrup into small saucepan. Blend in cornstarch until dissolved. Cook over medium heat, stirring constantly, until thickened. Stir in mustard and basil.

2. Thread meat, apricots, green pepper and mushrooms alternately onto skewers; brush with apricot syrup mixture. Grill kabobs over hot coals (or broil) about 5 minutes on each side or to desired doneness, brushing occasionally with additional syrup mixture. Garnish, if desired.
Makes 4 servings

Texas-Style Short Ribs

2 tablespoons chili powder
1 tablespoon LAWRY'S®
    Seasoned Salt
2 teaspoons LAWRY'S® Garlic
    Powder with Parsley
2 teaspoons ground cumin
1 teaspoon ground coriander
1/4 teaspoon hot pepper sauce
    (optional)
5 pounds trimmed beef short
    ribs
1 bottle (12 ounces) chili
    sauce
1 cup finely chopped onion
1 cup dry red wine
1/2 cup water
1/2 cup beef broth
1/2 cup olive oil

In small bowl, combine chili powder, Seasoned Salt, Garlic Powder with Parsley, cumin, coriander and hot pepper sauce, if desired; mix well. Rub both sides of ribs with spice mixture. Place in large resealable plastic food storage bag; refrigerate 1 hour. In medium bowl, combine remaining ingredients. Remove 1/2 cup marinade for basting. Add additional marinade to ribs; seal bag. Marinate in refrigerator at least 1 hour. Remove ribs; discard used marinade. Grill ribs over low heat 45 to 60 minutes or until tender, turning once and basting often with additional 1/2 cup marinade. *Do not baste during last 5 minutes of cooking.* Discard any remaining marinade.   *Makes 8 to 10 servings*

Serving Suggestion: Serve with coleslaw and potato wedges.

Hint: Ribs may be baked in 375°F. oven 45 to 60 minutes or until tender, turning once and basting often with additional 1/2 cup marinade.

Mexican Flank Steak

1/2 cup A.1.® Steak Sauce
1 (4-ounce) can diced green
    chiles
2 tablespoons lime juice*
1 (1½-pound) beef flank steak,
    lightly scored

Lemon juice may be substituted.

In blender or food processor, blend steak sauce, chiles and lime juice until smooth. Place steak in glass dish; coat with 1/2 cup chile mixture. Cover; chill 1 hour, turning occasionally.

Remove steak from marinade; reserve marinade. Grill steak over medium heat for 6 minutes on each side or until done, brushing often with reserved marinade. Thinly slice steak to serve.
    Makes 6 servings

Texas-Style Short Ribs

Cajun-Style Rubbed Steaks

⅓ cup **A.1.® Original or A.1.® Bold & Spicy Steak Sauce**
¼ cup **PARKAY® 70% Vegetable Oil Spread**, melted
¾ teaspoon each **garlic powder, onion powder and ground black pepper**
½ teaspoon **ground white pepper**
¼ teaspoon **ground red pepper**
4 (4- to 6-ounce) **beef shell steaks**, about ½ inch thick

In small bowl, blend steak sauce and spread; set aside.

In another small bowl, combine garlic powder, onion powder and peppers. Brush both sides of steaks with reserved steak sauce mixture, then sprinkle with seasoning mixture. Grill steaks over medium-high heat or broil 4 inches from heat source 5 minutes on each side or to desired doneness. Serve immediately. Garnish as desired.

Makes 4 servings

Tournedos with Mushroom Wine Sauce

¼ cup finely chopped **shallots**
2 tablespoons **PARKAY® 70% Vegetable Oil Spread**
¼ pound **small mushrooms**, halved
½ cup **A.1.® Steak Sauce**
¼ cup **Burgundy or other dry red wine**
¼ cup chopped **parsley**
4 (4-ounce) **beef tenderloin steaks (tournedos)**, about 1 inch thick

In medium saucepan, over medium heat, sauté shallots in spread until tender. Stir in mushrooms; sauté 1 minute. Stir in steak sauce and wine; heat to a boil. Reduce heat; simmer 10 minutes. Stir in parsley; keep warm.

Grill steaks over medium heat 10 to 12 minutes or until done, turning occasionally. Serve steaks topped with warm sauce.

Makes 4 servings

Cajun-Style Rubbed Steak

Ginger Beef and Pineapple Kabobs

1 cup LAWRY'S® Thai Ginger Marinade with Lime Juice, divided
1 can (16 ounces) pineapple chunks, juice reserved
1½ pounds sirloin steak, cut into 1½-inch cubes
2 red bell peppers, cut into chunks
2 medium onions, cut into wedges
Skewers

In large resealable plastic food storage bag, combine ½ cup Thai Ginger Marinade and 1 tablespoon pineapple juice; mix well. Add steak, bell peppers and onions; seal bag. Marinate in refrigerator at least 30 minutes. Remove steak and vegetables; discard used marinade. Alternately thread steak, vegetables and pineapple onto skewers. Grill or broil skewers 10 to 12 minutes or until desired doneness, turning once and basting often with additional ½ cup Thai Ginger Marinade. *Do not baste during last 5 minutes of cooking.* Discard any remaining marinade.   *Makes 6 servings*

Serving Suggestion: Serve kabobs with a light salad and bread.

Marinated Steak Ranchero

⅓ cup A.1.® Original or A.1.® Bold & Spicy Steak Sauce
⅓ cup purchased salsa
1 tablespoon lime juice
1 (1-pound) beef top round steak, about ¾ inch thick
⅓ cup sliced pitted ripe olives, divided
4 cups shredded lettuce
⅓ cup dairy sour cream

In small bowl, combine steak sauce, salsa and juice. Place steak in nonmetal dish; coat both sides with salsa mixture. Cover; refrigerate 1 hour, turning occasionally.

Remove steak from marinade; reserve marinade. In small saucepan, over medium heat, heat reserved marinade to a boil; simmer 5 minutes. Reserve 2 tablespoons olives for garnish. Stir remaining olives into marinade; keep warm.

Grill steak over medium heat or broil 6 inches from heat source 6 minutes on each side or to desired doneness. To serve, arrange lettuce on serving platter. Thinly slice steak across grain; arrange over lettuce. Top with warm sauce and dollop with sour cream. Garnish with reserved olives.   *Makes 4 servings*

Ginger Beef and Pineapple Kabobs

Grilled Meat Loaf

1½ pounds ground chuck or ground sirloin
½ cup seasoned dry bread crumbs
⅔ cup chili sauce, divided
⅓ cup grated onion
1 egg
½ teaspoon pepper
¼ teaspoon salt
2 tablespoons packed light brown sugar
1 tablespoon spicy brown or Dijon-style mustard

Prepare barbecue grill for direct cooking. Combine beef, bread crumbs, ⅓ cup chili sauce, onion, egg, pepper and salt in large bowl; mix well. On cutting board or cookie sheet, shape mixture into 9×5-inch oval loaf.

Combine remaining ⅓ cup chili sauce, sugar and mustard in small bowl; mix well. Set aside. Place meat loaf on grid. Grill meat loaf, on covered grill, over medium-hot coals 10 minutes. Carefully turn meat loaf over using 2 large spatulas.

Brush chili sauce mixture over top of meat loaf. Continue to grill, covered, 10 to 12 minutes for medium-well or until desired doneness is reached. (If desired, insert instant-read thermometer* into center of thickest part of meat loaf. Thermometer should register 160°F for medium-well.) Let stand 10 minutes before slicing. Serve with mashed potatoes and peas and carrots, if desired. *Makes 4 to 6 servings*

Do not leave instant-read thermometer in meat loaf during grilling since thermometer is not heatproof.

Grilled Steak au Poivre

½ cup A.1.® Steak Sauce, divided
1 (1½-pound) beef sirloin steak, ¾ inch thick
2 teaspoons cracked black pepper
½ cup dairy sour cream
2 tablespoons ketchup

Using 2 tablespoons steak sauce, brush both sides of steak; sprinkle 1 teaspoon pepper on each side, pressing into steak. Set aside.

In medium saucepan, over medium heat, combine remaining steak sauce, sour cream and ketchup. Cook and stir over low heat until heated through (do not boil); keep warm.

Grill steak over medium heat 5 minutes on each side or until done. Serve steak with warm sauce. *Makes 6 servings*

Grilled Meat Loaf

Guadalajara Beef

**1 bottle (12 ounces) Mexican
    dark beer***
¼ cup soy sauce
2 cloves garlic, minced
1 teaspoon ground cumin
1 teaspoon chili powder
1 teaspoon hot pepper sauce
**4 beef bottom sirloin steaks
    or boneless strip steaks
    (4 to 6 ounces each)**
Salt and black pepper
**Red, green and yellow bell
    peppers, cut lengthwise
    into quarters, seeded
    (optional)**
Salsa (recipe follows)
Flour tortillas (optional)
Lime wedges

Substitute any beer for Mexican dark beer.

Combine beer, soy sauce, garlic, cumin, chili powder and hot pepper sauce in large shallow glass dish or large heavy plastic food storage bag. Add beef; cover dish or close bag. Marinate in refrigerator up to 12 hours, turning beef several times. Remove beef from marinade; discard marinade. Season with salt and pepper.

Oil hot grid to help prevent sticking. Grill beef and bell peppers, if desired, on covered grill, over medium KINGSFORD® Briquets, 8 to 12 minutes, turning once. Beef should be of medium doneness and peppers should be tender. Serve with salsa, tortillas, if desired, and lime.   *Makes 4 servings*

Salsa

2 cups coarsely chopped seeded tomatoes
2 green onions with tops, sliced
1 clove garlic, minced
**1 to 2 teaspoons minced seeded jalapeño or serrano
    chili pepper, fresh or canned**
1 tablespoon olive or vegetable oil
2 to 3 teaspoons lime juice
8 to 10 sprigs fresh cilantro, minced (optional)
½ teaspoon salt or to taste
½ teaspoon sugar or to taste
¼ teaspoon black pepper

Combine tomatoes, green onions, garlic, chili pepper, oil and lime juice in medium bowl. Stir in cilantro, if desired. Season with salt, sugar and black pepper. Adjust seasonings to taste, adding lime juice or chili pepper, if desired.   *Makes about 2 cups*

Guadalajara Beef

Mushroom-Sauced Steak

½ cup sliced onion
2 tablespoons **PARKAY® 70%
    Vegetable Oil Spread**
1½ cups **sliced mushrooms**
1 cup **A.1.® Bold & Spicy Steak
    Sauce**
½ cup **dairy sour cream**
2 **(8-ounce) beef club or strip
    steaks, about 1 inch thick**

In medium skillet, over medium heat, sauté onion in spread until tender, about 5 minutes. Add mushrooms; sauté 5 minutes more. Stir in steak sauce; heat to a boil. Reduce heat and simmer 5 minutes; stir in sour cream. Cook and stir until heated through (do not boil); keep warm.

Grill steaks over medium heat 5 minutes on each side or until done. Serve steaks topped with mushroom sauce.

Makes 4 servings

Grilled Peppered London Broil

1¼ cups **canned crushed
    tomatoes**
1 medium **onion, quartered**
1 tablespoon **FILIPPO BERIO®
    Olive Oil**
1 tablespoon **cider vinegar**
1 jalapeño **pepper, seeded and
    chopped** *or* 1 **tablespoon
    purchased chopped hot
    pepper**
1 clove **garlic**
½ teaspoon **salt**
1 teaspoon **freshly ground
    black pepper**
1 **(2-pound) beef London
    broil, 2 inches thick**

Process tomatoes, onion, olive oil, vinegar, jalapeño pepper and garlic in blender container or food processor until smooth. Transfer mixture to small saucepan. Bring to a boil. Reduce heat to low; simmer 2 minutes. Pour marinade into shallow glass dish. Stir in salt and black pepper. Cool slightly. Add London broil to marinade; turn to coat both sides. Cover; marinate in refrigerator at least 4 hours or overnight, turning occasionally. Remove London broil, reserving marinade.

Brush barbecue grid with olive oil. Grill London broil, on covered grill, over hot coals 8 to 10 minutes, brushing frequently with reserved marinade. Turn with tongs. Grill an additional 18 to 20 minutes for medium-rare or until desired doneness is reached.

Makes 6 to 8 servings

Mushroom-Sauced Steak

Pepper-Spiced Beef Skewers and Beans

1½ pounds tender, lean beef
  such as tenderloin
1 large red bell pepper
1 large green bell pepper
1 large onion, halved
  Pepper-Spice Seasoning
  (recipe follows)
2 tablespoons lemon juice
2 teaspoons olive oil
3 cups cooked and drained,
  Great Northern, navy or
  pinto beans *or* 2 cans
  (16 ounces each) beans,
  rinsed and drained
1 can (28 ounces) no-salt-
  added stewed tomatoes,
  drained
2 tablespoons firmly packed
  brown sugar
2 tablespoons chopped fresh
  parsley

Cut beef into ¾- to 1-inch cubes. Cut peppers and half of onion into ¾- to 1-inch squares (you will need 24 to 30 squares of each). Thread meat and vegetables alternately onto 6 (10- to 12-inch) metal skewers beginning with 1 piece of each vegetable followed by 1 cube meat. Combine 2 tablespoons Pepper-Spice Seasoning with lemon juice in small bowl. Brush mixture over beef cubes.

Spray cold grid with nonstick cooking spray. Adjust grid 4 to 6 inches above heat. Preheat grill to medium-high heat. Grill skewers 8 to 10 minutes, turning every 2 to 3 minutes, or until meat is grilled to desired doneness.

Meanwhile, finely chop remaining onion half. Heat oil in medium saucepan over medium-high heat. Add onion and remaining 2 tablespoons spice mixture. Cook and stir 3 minutes or until onion is tender (do not let spices burn). Stir in beans, tomatoes and brown sugar. Cover; cook and stir until heated through. Stir in parsley.

Makes 6 servings

Pepper-Spice Seasoning

2 tablespoons lemon juice
2 tablespoons pressed or minced garlic
2 teaspoons dried oregano leaves, crushed
2 teaspoons black pepper
1 teaspoon ground cumin
1 teaspoon ground allspice

Combine all ingredients in small bowl; stir to combine.

Tip: As a good source of protein and fiber, beans are hard to beat. There are about 5 grams of protein and almost 6 grams of fiber in a ⅓-cup portion of beans. What is more, they have no cholesterol and only a trace of fat.

Pepper-Spiced Beef Skewers and Beans

Picadillo-Stuffed Papayas

½ cup **LAWRY'S®** Mesquite
   Marinade with Lime Juice
½ **pound flank steak**
 1 **tablespoon vegetable oil**
½ **cup chopped green bell**
   pepper
½ **cup chopped onion**
½ **cup chopped tomato**
¼ **cup sliced pimiento-stuffed**
   olives
 2 **tablespoons raisins**
½ **teaspoon LAWRY'S®**
   Seasoned Pepper
 2 **ripe papayas, halved and**
   seeded

In large resealable plastic food storage bag, combine Mesquite Marinade and steak; seal bag. Marinate in refrigerator at least 30 minutes. Remove steak; discard used marinade. Grill or broil steak 10 to 12 minutes or until desired doneness, turning halfway through grilling time. Thinly slice steak on the diagonal across the grain. In large skillet, heat oil; add bell pepper and onion and cook over medium-high heat until tender. Add tomato, olives, raisins, Seasoned Pepper and steak; cook until heated throughout. Fill papayas with steak mixture.
Makes 4 servings

Serving Suggestion: Serve with hot cooked couscous.

Hint: Papayas may be peeled, if desired.

Fruit Glazed Beef Ribs

 4 **pounds beef back ribs, cut**
   into individual ribs
⅓ **cup A.1.® Bold & Spicy Steak**
   Sauce
¼ **cup ketchup**
¼ **cup apricot preserves**
 1 **tablespoon lemon juice**
½ **teaspoon grated lemon peel**

Arrange ribs on rack in large roasting pan. Bake at 400°F for 30 minutes.

In small saucepan, over medium heat, cook and stir steak sauce, ketchup, preserves, lemon juice and lemon peel until blended. Grill ribs over medium heat for 20 minutes or until done, turning and brushing often with prepared sauce. Serve hot.
Makes 6 to 8 servings

Picadillo-Stuffed Papayas

Savory Grilled Tournedos

⅓ cup **A.1.® Steak Sauce**
¼ cup **ketchup**
¼ cup **orange marmalade**
2 tablespoons **lemon juice**
2 tablespoons **minced onion**
1 clove **garlic, crushed**
8 slices **bacon (about 5 ounces)**
8 (4-ounce) **beef tenderloin steaks (tournedos), about 1 inch thick**
Mushroom halves, radishes and parsley sprigs for garnish

In small bowl, blend steak sauce, ketchup, marmalade, lemon juice, onion and garlic; set aside.

Wrap a bacon slice around edge of each steak; secure with string or wooden toothpick. Grill steaks over medium-high heat for 10 minutes or to desired doneness, turning occasionally and brushing often with ½ cup prepared sauce. Remove string or toothpicks; serve steaks with remaining sauce. Garnish with mushroom halves, radishes and parsley, if desired. *Makes 8 servings*

Roscoe's Ribs

1 to 2 tablespoons **LAWRY'S® Seasoned Salt**
5 pounds **beef or pork ribs**
1 cup **Worcestershire sauce**
¾ cup **apple cider vinegar**
1 tablespoon **olive oil**
½ teaspoon **minced garlic**

Sprinkle Seasoned Salt over ribs. In large resealable plastic food storage bag, combine Worcestershire, vinegar, oil and garlic; mix well. Remove at least ½ cup marinade for basting. Add ribs; seal bag. Marinate in refrigerator at least 1 hour. Remove ribs; discard used marinade. Grill over low heat or bake ribs in 350°F. oven 1 to 1¼ hours or until no longer pink, turning and basting often with additional ½ cup marinade. *Makes 4 to 6 servings*

Hint: For extra flavor, marinate ribs overnight.

Savory Grilled Tournedo

Fajitas

Fajita Marinade (page 151)
1 pound flank steak
6 (10-inch) flour tortillas _or_ 12 (7-inch) flour tortillas
4 bell peppers, any color, halved
1 large bunch green onions
Salsa Cruda (page 151)
1 cup coarsely chopped fresh cilantro
1 ripe avocado, thinly sliced (optional)
6 tablespoons low-fat sour cream (optional)

1. Combine Fajita Marinade and flank steak in resealable plastic food storage bag. Press air from bag and seal. Refrigerate 30 minutes or up to 24 hours.

2. Place tortillas in stacks of 3. Wrap each stack in foil; set aside.

3. Drain marinade from meat into small saucepan. Bring to a boil over high heat. Remove from heat.

4. Spray cold grid of grill with nonstick cooking spray. Adjust grid 4 to 6 inches above heat. Preheat grill to medium-high heat. Place meat in center of grid. Place bell peppers, skin side down, around meat; cover. Grill bell peppers 6 minutes or until skin is spotted brown. Turn over and continue grilling 6 to 8 minutes or until tender. Move to sides of grill to keep warm while meat finishes grilling.

5. Continue to grill meat, basting frequently with marinade, 8 minutes or until browned on bottom. Turn over; grill 8 to 10 minutes or until slightly pink in center.

6. During the last 4 minutes of grilling, brush green onions with remaining marinade and place on grid; grill 1 to 2 minutes or until browned in spots. Turn over; grill 1 to 2 minutes or until tender.

7. Place packets of tortillas on grid; heat about 5 minutes. Slice bell peppers and onions into thin 2-inch-long pieces. Thinly slice meat across the grain.

8. Place each tortilla on plate. Place meat, peppers, onions, Salsa Cruda and cilantro in center of each tortilla. Fold bottom 3 inches of each tortilla up over filling; fold sides completely over filling to enclose. Serve with avocado and sour cream, if desired.

Makes 6 servings

Cook's Tip: Bell peppers are naturally delicious and grilling them at medium-high heat gives them a wonderful new flavor without adding any fat.

Fajita Marinade

½ cup lime juice *or* ¼ cup lime juice and ¼ cup tequilla or beer
1 tablespoon dried oregano leaves
1 tablespoon minced garlic
2 teaspoons ground cumin
2 teaspoons black pepper

1. Combine lime juice, oregano, garlic, cumin and black pepper in 1-cup glass measure.

Salsa Cruda

1 cup chopped tomato
2 tablespoons minced onion
2 tablespoons minced fresh cilantro (optional)
2 tablespoons lime juice
½ jalapeño pepper, seeded and minced
1 clove garlic, minced

1. Combine tomato, onion, cilantro, lime juice, jalapeño pepper and garlic in small bowl.

Smoke-Cooked Beef Ribs

**Wood chunks or chips for
  smoking
4 to 6 pounds beef back ribs,
  cut into slabs of 3 to 4 ribs
  each
Salt and black pepper
1⅓ cups K.C. MASTERPIECE®
  Barbecue Sauce, divided
Beer at room temperature
  or hot tap water
Grilled corn-on-the-cob
  (optional)**

Soak 4 wood chunks or several handfuls of wood chips in water; drain. Spread ribs on baking sheet or tray; season with salt and pepper. Brush with half of sauce. Let stand at cool room temperature up to 30 minutes.

Arrange low KINGSFORD® Briquets on each side of rectangular metal or foil drip pan. (Since the ribs have been brushed with sauce before cooking, low heat is needed to keep them moist.) Pour in beer to fill pan half full. Add soaked wood (all the chunks; part of chips) to fire.

Oil hot grid to help prevent sticking. Place ribs on grid, meaty side up, directly above drip pan. Smoke-cook ribs, on covered grill, about 1 hour, brushing remaining sauce over ribs 2 or 3 times during cooking. If grill has thermometer, maintain cooking temperature between 250°F to 275°F. Add a few more briquets after 30 minutes, or as necessary, to maintain constant temperature. Add more soaked wood chips every 30 minutes, if necessary. Serve with grilled corn-on-the-cob, if desired.

Makes 4 to 6 servings

Beef Saté Strips

**¾ cup A.1.® Steak Sauce
⅓ cup chunky peanut butter
2 tablespoons teriyaki sauce
1 (1-pound) beef flank steak,
  thinly sliced
1 cup (1-inch) green onion
  pieces (about 1 bunch)
½ cup beef broth
1 teaspoon cornstarch
5 lime wedges, for garnish
Hot cooked rice**

In small bowl, combine steak sauce, peanut butter and teriyaki sauce. Place steak strips in glass dish; coat with ⅔ cup prepared steak sauce mixture. Cover; chill 1 hour, stirring occasionally.

Soak 5 (12-inch) wooden skewers in water for at least 30 minutes. Remove steak strips from marinade. Alternately thread steak strips and onion pieces onto skewers. Grill over medium heat 6 to 8 minutes or until done, turning occasionally. Meanwhile, in small saucepan, over medium heat, cook and stir remaining steak sauce mixture, beef broth and cornstarch until mixture thickens and begins to boil. Garnish steak with lime wedges. Serve over rice with prepared sauce.

Makes 5 servings

Smoke-Cooked Beef Ribs

Spicy Orange Beef and Broccoli Kabobs

1 (1-pound) boneless beef top sirloin steak, cut into 1-inch cubes
1 medium onion, cut into wedges
1 cup broccoli flowerettes, blanched
3 medium carrots, sliced diagonally, blanched
½ cup A.1.® Thick & Hearty Steak Sauce
¼ cup thawed frozen orange juice concentrate
1 tablespoon firmly packed brown sugar
½ to 1 teaspoon crushed red pepper flakes
Hot cooked rice or noodles

Soak 8 (10-inch) wooden skewers in water at least 30 minutes.

Alternately thread steak, onion, broccoli and carrots onto skewers. In small saucepan, over high heat, heat steak sauce, juice concentrate, sugar and pepper flakes to a boil. Brush kabobs with steak sauce mixture. Grill kabobs over medium heat or broil 6 inches from heat source 8 to 10 minutes or until steak is desired doneness, turning and basting with steak sauce mixture occasionally. (Discard any remaining steak sauce mixture.) Serve immediately with rice or noodles. Garnish as desired.

Makes 4 servings

Hot Off The Grill

Turn small cuts of meat such as kabobs, burgers and steaks halfway through grilling.

Spicy Orange Beef and Broccoli Kabobs

Vietnamese Loin Steaks with Black Bean Relish

**1 stalk lemongrass, outer
    leaves removed and upper
    stalk trimmed**
1 tablespoon sugar
1 tablespoon fish sauce
1 teaspoon minced garlic
1/2 to 1 teaspoon hot chili oil
**2 boneless beef top loin steaks
    (8 ounces each), about
    1 inch thick**
**1 can (about 8 3/4 ounces)
    whole baby corn (about 8
    cobs), rinsed and drained**
**1 can (about 15 ounces) black
    beans, rinsed and drained**
1 cup diced mango
**1/2 green bell pepper, cut into
    strips**
**2 tablespoons chopped red
    onion**
**1 jalapeño pepper,* seeded
    and sliced (optional)**
Juice of 1/2 lemon
1/2 teaspoon vegetable oil
1/2 teaspoon honey
1/8 teaspoon salt

*Jalapeños can sting and irritate the skin; wear
rubber gloves when handling and do not touch
eyes. Wash hands after handling.*

1. Flatten lemongrass with meat mallet and mince. Combine with sugar, fish sauce, garlic and chili oil in baking dish. Cut each steak lengthwise into 2 strips. Place in dish with marinade, coating both sides. Cover; refrigerate 1 hour, turning once.

2. Halve corn cobs diagonally; combine with beans, mango, bell pepper, onion and jalapeño, if desired, in large bowl. Combine lemon juice, oil, honey and salt in small bowl; stir into bean mixture.

3. Grill steaks on covered grill over medium-hot coals 10 minutes for medium-rare or until desired doneness is reached, turning once. Serve with relish.

Makes 4 servings

Hot Off The Grill

To check the temperature of the coals, cautiously hold the palm of your hand at grid level—over the coals for direct heat—and count the number of seconds you can hold your hand in that position before the heat forces you to pull away. For a medium-hot grill (about 350°F to 375°F), you should be able to hold your hand there for 3 seconds.

Vietnamese Loin Steak with Black Bean Relish

Gazpacho Steak Roll

1 (2-pound) beef flank steak, butterflied
⅔ cup A.1.® Steak Sauce, divided
1 cup (4 ounces) shredded Monterey Jack cheese
½ cup chopped tomato
⅓ cup chopped cucumber
¼ cup chopped green bell pepper
2 tablespoons sliced green onion

Open butterflied steak like a book on smooth surface and flatten slightly. Spread ⅓ cup steak sauce over surface. Layer remaining ingredients over sauce. Roll up steak from short edge; secure with wooden toothpicks or tie with string if necessary.

Grill steak roll over medium heat 30 to 40 minutes or to desired doneness, turning and brushing often with remaining steak sauce during last 10 minutes of cooking. Remove toothpicks; slice and serve garnished as desired. *Makes 8 servings*

Perfectly Grilled Steak & Potatoes

Olive oil
1½ teaspoons cracked black pepper
2 cloves garlic, pressed
Salt
½ teaspoon dried thyme leaves
4 beef tenderloin steaks or boneless top loin steaks, 1½ inches thick
4 medium potatoes, cut into ½-inch slices
Ground black pepper
Lime wedges

Combine 2 tablespoons oil, cracked pepper, garlic, ½ teaspoon salt and thyme in cup. Brush oil mixture over steaks to coat both sides. Brush potato slices with additional oil; season to taste with additional salt and ground pepper. Lightly oil hot grid to prevent sticking. Grill beef on covered grill over medium-hot KINGSFORD® Briquets 10 to 12 minutes for medium-rare or to desired doneness, turning once. Grill potatoes 10 to 12 minutes or until golden brown and tender, turning once. Serve steaks with potatoes and lime wedges. *Makes 4 servings*

Gazpacho Steak Roll

Southwest Steak

¾ cup Italian dressing
½ cup minced fresh parsley
⅓ cup FRANK'S® Original
   REDHOT® Cayenne
   Pepper Sauce
3 tablespoons lime juice
1 tablespoon FRENCH'S®
   Worcestershire Sauce
2 pounds boneless sirloin or
   top round steak
   (1½ inches thick)

1. Place dressing, parsley, RedHot® sauce, juice and Worcestershire in blender or food processor. Cover; process until smooth. Reserve ⅔ cup sauce. Pour remaining sauce over steak in deep dish. Cover; refrigerate 30 minutes.

2. Grill or broil steak 8 minutes per side for medium-rare or to desired doneness. Let stand 5 minutes. Slice steak and serve with reserved sauce.

Makes 6 to 8 servings

Prep Time: *10 minutes*
Marinate Time: *30 minutes*
Cook Time: *20 minutes*

Hearty Grilled Tenderloins

2 cups sliced onions
2 tablespoons PARKAY® 70%
   Vegetable Oil Spread
1 (8-ounce) can peeled
   tomatoes, drained and
   chopped
½ cup A.1.® Steak Sauce,
   divided
2 tablespoons red wine
   vinegar
¼ cup chopped parsley
4 (4- to 6-ounce) beef
   tenderloin steaks, about
   1 inch thick

In medium saucepan, over medium-high heat, cook onions in spread until tender. Add tomatoes, ¼ cup steak sauce and vinegar; heat to a boil. Reduce heat; simmer 5 minutes. Remove from heat; stir in parsley. Keep warm.

Grill steaks over medium heat 5 minutes on each side or until done, brushing with remaining steak sauce. Serve steaks with warm sauce.

Makes 4 servings

Southwest Steak

Guadalajara Beef

1 bottle (12 ounces) dark beer
¼ cup low-sodium soy sauce
3 cloves garlic, minced
1 teaspoon ground cumin
1 teaspoon ground chili
    powder
½ teaspoon ground red pepper
1 pound beef flank steak
6 medium red, yellow or
    green bell peppers, seeded
    and cut lengthwise into
    quarters
8 (6- to 8-inch) flour tortillas
    Sour cream
    Salsa

1. Combine beer, soy sauce, garlic, cumin, chili powder and red pepper in resealable plastic food storage bag; knead bag to combine. Add beef and seal. Refrigerate up to 24 hours, turning occasionally.

2. To complete recipe, remove beef from marinade; discard remaining marinade. Grill beef over hot coals 7 minutes per side or until desired doneness. Grill bell peppers 7 to 10 minutes or until tender, turning once.

3. Slice beef and serve with bell peppers, tortillas, sour cream and salsa.
Makes 4 servings

Make-Ahead Time: *Up to 1 day before serving*
Final Prep Time: *20 minutes*

Tijuana Blackened Steak

¾ teaspoon garlic powder
¾ teaspoon onion powder
¾ teaspoon ground black
    pepper
½ teaspoon ground white
    pepper
¼ teaspoon ground red pepper
4 (4- to 6-ounce) beef shell or
    strip steaks, about ½ inch
    thick
½ cup A.1.® Steak Sauce
¼ cup PARKAY® 70% Vegetable
    Oil Spread, melted

In small bowl, combine garlic powder, onion powder and peppers; spread on waxed paper. Coat both sides of steaks with seasoning mixture.

In small bowl, combine steak sauce and spread. Grill steaks 10 to 15 minutes or until done, turning and brushing often with ¼ cup steak sauce mixture. Serve steaks with remaining steak sauce mixture.
Makes 4 servings

Guadalajara Beef

Pesto Beef Swirls

½ cup A.1.® Original or A.1.®
   Bold & Spicy Steak Sauce
¼ cup grated Parmesan
   cheese
¼ cup pignoli (pine nuts) or
   walnuts
¼ cup fresh parsley leaves
 2 tablespoons dried basil
   leaves
 2 cloves garlic
 1 (2-pound) beef flank steak,
   pounded to ½-inch
   thickness
   Additional A.1.® Original or
   A.1.® Bold & Spicy Steak
   Sauce (optional)

In blender or food processor, blend steak sauce, cheese, pignoli, parsley, basil and garlic to a coarse paste; spread over top of steak. Cut steak across grain into eight 1-inch-wide strips. Roll up each strip from short edge; secure with wooden toothpicks. Grill steak strips over medium heat or broil 6 inches from heat source 7 to 8 minutes on each side or to desired doneness, basting frequently with additional steak sauce if desired. Remove toothpicks. Serve immediately. Garnish as desired.   *Makes 4 to 8 servings*

Hot Off The Grill

To light a charcoal fire, arrange the coals in a pyramid shape 20 to 30 minutes prior to cooking. The pyramid shape provides enough ventilation for the coals to catch. To start with lighter fluid, soak the coals with about ½ cup fluid, wait one minute to allow the fluid to soak into the coals and light with a match.

Pesto Beef Swirls

Teriyaki Steak Strip Kabobs

½ cup A.1.® Original or A.1.®
   Bold & Spicy Steak Sauce
2 tablespoons soy sauce
2 tablespoons firmly packed
   light brown sugar
2 cloves garlic, minced
1 teaspoon grated fresh
   ginger
1 (1-pound) boneless beef
   sirloin steak, about 1 inch
   thick, thinly sliced
2 cups broccoli flowerettes,
   blanched
2 cups fresh mushroom caps
   (about 16 mushrooms)
1 cup pineapple chunks
2 tablespoons sesame seed,
   toasted
   Hot cooked rice

Soak 8 (10-inch) wooden skewers in water at least 30 minutes.

In small bowl, combine steak sauce, soy sauce, sugar, garlic and ginger. Place steak in nonmetal dish; coat with steak sauce mixture. Cover; refrigerate 1 hour, stirring occasionally.

Remove steak from marinade; discard marinade. Alternately thread steak, broccoli, mushrooms and pineapple onto skewers. Grill kabobs over medium heat or broil 6 inches from heat source 5 to 8 minutes or until steak is desired doneness, turning occasionally. Sprinkle kabobs with sesame seed. Serve immediately with rice. Garnish as desired.

Makes 4 servings

Hot Off The Grill

To avoid flare-ups and charred food when grilling, remove visible fat from meat before grilling.

Teriyaki Steak Strip Kabobs

Chili-Beer Glazed Steak

⅔ cup **A.1.® Original** or **A.1.®**
   Bold & Spicy Steak Sauce
½ cup **chili sauce**
½ cup **chopped green onions**
⅓ cup **beer**
2 tablespoons **chopped fresh**
   cilantro
¼ teaspoon **crushed red**
   pepper flakes
1 (2-pound) **beef flank steak**

In small bowl, combine steak sauce, chili sauce, green onions, beer, cilantro and pepper flakes; reserve ½ cup for basting steak.

In small saucepan, over medium heat, heat remaining steak sauce mixture to a boil; keep warm.

Grill steak over medium heat or broil 6 inches from heat source 6 minutes on each side or to desired doneness, basting often with ½ cup basting sauce. Thinly slice steak across grain; serve with warm sauce. Garnish as desired.   *Makes 8 servings*

Stuffed Salisbury Steak with Mushroom & Onion Topping

2 pounds **ground beef**
¼ cup **FRENCH'S®**
   Worcestershire Sauce
2⅔ cups **FRENCH'S® French**
   Fried Onions, divided
1 teaspoon **garlic salt**
½ teaspoon **ground black**
   pepper
4 ounces **Cheddar cheese, cut**
   into 6 sticks (about
   2 × ½ × ½ inches)
   Mushroom Topping (recipe
   follows)

Combine beef, Worcestershire, 1⅓ cups French Fried Onions, garlic salt and pepper. Divide meat evenly into 6 portions. Place 1 stick cheese in center of each portion, firmly pressing and shaping meat into ovals around cheese.

Place steaks on grid. Grill over medium-high coals 15 minutes or until meat thermometer inserted into beef reaches 160°F, turning once. Serve with Mushroom Topping and sprinkle with remaining 1⅓ cups onions.   *Makes 6 servings*

Mushroom Topping

2 tablespoons **butter or margarine**
1 package (12 ounces) **mushrooms, wiped clean and**
   quartered
2 tablespoons **FRENCH'S® Worcestershire Sauce**

Melt butter in large skillet over medium-high heat. Add mushrooms; cook 5 minutes or until browned, stirring often. Add Worcestershire. Reduce heat to low. Cook 5 minutes, stirring occasionally.   *Makes 6 servings*

Chili-Beer Glazed Steak

Fajitas with Avocado Salsa

1 beef flank steak (1¼ to 1½
    pounds)
¼ cup tequila or nonalcoholic
    beer
3 tablespoons fresh lime juice
1 tablespoon seeded and
    minced jalapeño pepper*
2 large cloves garlic, minced
1 large red bell pepper
1 large green bell pepper
    Avocado Salsa (page 171)
8 flour tortillas (6- to 7-inch
    diameter)
4 slices red onion, cut ¼ inch
    thick

*Jalapeño peppers can sting and irritate the skin;
wear rubber gloves when handling peppers and
do not touch eyes. Wash hands after handling
peppers.

1. Place steak in large resealable plastic food storage bag. Combine tequila, lime juice, jalapeño and garlic in small bowl; pour over steak. Seal bag tightly, turning to coat. Marinate in refrigerator 1 to 4 hours, turning once.

2. Stand peppers on end on cutting board. Cut off sides into 4 lengthwise slices with utility knife. (Cut close to, but not through, stem.) Discard stem and seeds. Rinse inside of peppers under cold running water. Set aside.

3. Prepare barbecue grill for direct cooking.

4. Meanwhile, prepare Avocado Salsa.

5. Wrap tortillas in heavy-duty foil.

6. Drain steak; discard marinade. Place steak, bell peppers and onion slices on grid. Grill, on covered grill, over medium-hot coals 14 to 18 minutes for medium or until desired doneness is reached, turning steak, bell peppers and onion slices halfway through grilling time. Place tortilla packet on grid during last 5 to 7 minutes of grilling; turn halfway through grilling time to heat through.

7. Transfer steak to carving board. Carve steak across the grain into thin slices. Slice bell peppers into thin strips. Separate onion slices into rings. Divide among tortillas; roll up and top with Avocado Salsa.

Makes 4 servings

Avocado Salsa

1 large ripe avocado, halved
  and pitted
1 large tomato, seeded and
  diced
3 tablespoons chopped
  cilantro
1 tablespoon vegetable oil
1 tablespoon fresh lime juice
2 teaspoons minced fresh or
  drained, bottled jalapeño
  pepper
1 clove garlic, minced
½ teaspoon salt

1. Scoop avocado flesh from shells with large spoon; place on cutting board. Coarsely chop avocado flesh into ½-inch cubes. Transfer to medium bowl.

2. Gently stir in tomato, cilantro, oil, lime juice, jalapeño, garlic and salt until well combined. Let stand at room temperature while grilling steak. Cover; refrigerate if preparing in advance. Bring to room temperature before serving.   *Makes about 1½ cups*

South-of-the-Border Kabobs

5 cloves garlic
½ cup A.1.® Original or A.1.®
  Bold & Spicy Steak Sauce
¼ cup PARKAY® 70% Vegetable
  Oil Spread, melted
1 tablespoon finely chopped
  fresh cilantro
¾ teaspoon ground cumin
⅛ teaspoon ground red pepper
1 (1½-pound) beef flank steak,
  thinly sliced across grain
2 small zucchini, cut
  lengthwise into thin slices
3 medium plum tomatoes, cut
  into ½-inch slices
¾ cup baby carrots, blanched
  Hot cooked rice or noodles

Soak 8 (10-inch) wooden skewers in water at least 30 minutes.

Mince 1 clove garlic; halve remaining cloves and set aside. In small bowl, combine steak sauce, PARKAY® 70% Vegetable Oil Spread, cilantro, minced garlic, cumin and pepper; set aside.

Alternately thread steak strips and zucchini (accordion style), reserved garlic, tomatoes and carrots onto skewers. Grill kabobs over medium heat or broil 6 inches from heat source 10 to 12 minutes or until steak is desired doneness, turning and basting often with reserved steak sauce mixture. (Discard any remaining steak sauce mixture.) Serve immediately with rice.

Makes 4 servings

Rosemary Steak

**4 boneless top loin beef steaks
   or New York strip steaks
   (about 6 ounces each)**
**2 tablespoons minced fresh
   rosemary**
2 cloves garlic, minced
**1 tablespoon extra-virgin olive
   oil**
1 teaspoon grated lemon peel
**1 teaspoon coarsely ground
   black pepper**
**½ teaspoon salt
   Fresh rosemary sprigs**

Score steaks in diamond pattern on both sides. Combine minced rosemary, garlic, oil, lemon peel, pepper and salt in small bowl; rub mixture onto surface of meat. Cover and refrigerate at least 15 minutes. Grill steaks over medium-hot KINGSFORD® Briquets about 4 minutes per side until medium-rare or to desired doneness. Cut steaks diagonally into ½-inch-thick slices. Garnish with rosemary sprigs. *Makes 4 servings*

Marinated Moroccan Beef

**⅓ cup A.1.® Thick & Hearty
   Steak Sauce**
**2 tablespoons red wine
   vinegar**
2 tablespoons vegetable oil
1 teaspoon chili powder
**1 teaspoon dried oregano
   leaves**
**½ teaspoon coarsely ground
   black pepper**
½ teaspoon ground cinnamon
2 cloves garlic, minced
**1 (1½- to 2-pound) beef top
   round steak, about 1 inch
   thick**

In small bowl, combine steak sauce, vinegar, oil, chili powder, oregano, pepper, cinnamon and garlic. Place steak in nonmetal dish; coat with steak sauce mixture. Cover; refrigerate 1 hour, turning occasionally.

Remove steak from marinade; reserve marinade. Grill steak over medium heat or broil 6 inches from heat source 25 to 35 minutes or to desired doneness, turning often. In small saucepan, over high heat, heat reserved marinade to a boil; simmer 5 minutes or until thickened. Thinly slice beef; serve with warm sauce.

Makes 6 servings

Rosemary Steak

Jamaican Steak

2 pounds beef flank steak
¼ cup packed brown sugar
3 tablespoons orange juice
3 tablespoons lime juice
3 cloves garlic, minced
1 piece (1½×1 inches) fresh
    ginger, minced
2 teaspoons grated orange
    peel
2 teaspoons grated lime peel
1 teaspoon salt
1 teaspoon black pepper
¼ teaspoon ground cinnamon
⅛ teaspoon ground cloves
    Shredded orange peel
    Shredded lime peel

Score both sides of beef.* Combine sugar, juices, garlic, ginger, grated peels, salt, pepper, cinnamon and cloves in 2-quart glass dish. Add beef; turn to coat. Cover and refrigerate steak at least 2 hours. Remove beef from marinade; discard marinade. Grill beef over medium-hot KINGSFORD® Briquets about 6 minutes per side until medium-rare or to desired doneness. Garnish with shredded orange and lime peels. *Makes 6 servings*

To score flank steak, cut ¼-inch-deep diagonal lines about 1 inch apart in surface of steak to form diamond-shaped design.

Grilled Steak with Blue Cheese Sauce

½ cup heavy cream
½ cup A.1.® Original or A.1.®
    Bold & Spicy Steak Sauce,
    divided
¾ cup crumbled blue cheese
    (3 ounces), divided
1 tablespoon all-purpose flour
1 (1- to 1¼-pound) beef top
    round steak, about 1 inch
    thick
¼ cup sliced green onions

In small saucepan, over medium heat, heat cream, 6 tablespoons steak sauce, ½ cup cheese and flour, stirring constantly until cheese melts and mixture begins to boil; keep warm.

Grill steak over medium heat 7 minutes on each side or to desired doneness, basting occasionally with remaining 2 tablespoons steak sauce. Slice steak; serve topped with warm sauce, remaining ¼ cup cheese and green onions.

Makes 5 servings

Jamaican Steak

Pineapple Teriyaki Marinated Steak

1 (8-ounce) can sliced pineapple in its own juice, drained (reserve juice)
½ cup A.1.® Thick & Hearty Steak Sauce
3 tablespoons teriyaki sauce
1 teaspoon ground ginger
1 (1½-pound) beef flank or top round steak, lightly scored

In small bowl, combine reserved juice, steak sauce, teriyaki sauce and ginger. Place steak in nonmetal dish; coat with steak sauce mixture. Cover; refrigerate 1 hour, turning occasionally.

Remove steak from marinade; reserve marinade. Grill steak over medium-high heat or broil 4 inches from heat source 15 to 20 minutes or to desired doneness, turning and basting with marinade occasionally. Grill or broil pineapple slices 1 minute, turning once. In small saucepan, over high heat, heat reserved marinade to a boil; simmer 5 minutes or until thickened. Slice steak across grain; serve with pineapple slices and warm sauce. Garnish as desired.

Makes 6 servings

Hot Off The Grill

To check the temperature of the coals, cautiously hold the palm of your hand at grid level—over the coals for direct heat—and count the number of seconds you can hold your hand in that position before the heat forces you to pull away. For a medium grill (about 300°F to 350°F), you should be able to hold your hand there for 4 seconds.

Pineapple Teriyaki Marinated Steak

Zesty Peppered Steaks

4 ounces light cream cheese
½ cup A.1.® Original or A.1.®
Bold & Spicy Steak Sauce,
divided
1 tablespoon prepared
horseradish
4 (4-ounce) beef rib eye
steaks, about ¾ inch thick
2 teaspoons coarsely ground
black pepper

In small saucepan, over medium heat, stir cream cheese, ¼ cup steak sauce and horseradish until heated through; keep warm.

Brush both sides of steaks with 2 tablespoons steak sauce, dividing evenly. Sprinkle ¼ teaspoon pepper on each side of each steak, pressing into meat and sauce. Grill steaks over medium-high heat or broil 4 inches from heat source 4 minutes on each side or to desired doneness, basting occasionally with remaining 2 tablespoons steak sauce. Serve with warm sauce. Garnish as desired. *Makes 4 servings*

Grilled Caribbean Steaks

6 tablespoons brown sugar
2½ tablespoons paprika
2 tablespoons granulated
sugar
1 tablespoon kosher salt
1 tablespoon chili powder
1¼ teaspoons granulated garlic
or garlic powder
1¼ teaspoons dried oregano
leaves
1¼ teaspoons dried basil leaves
¾ teaspoon dried thyme leaves
¾ teaspoon celery seed
¼ teaspoon cayenne pepper
2 lean beef T-bone steaks
(12 to 16 ounces each), 1
inch thick

To prepare spice mix, combine all ingredients except steak in small bowl; mix well. Measure out ¼ cup spice mix, reserving remaining for other uses.* Rub steaks with ¼ cup spice mix, using 1 tablespoon per side. Refrigerate steaks, covered, overnight or up to 3 days. Grill steaks on covered grill over medium KINGSFORD® Briquets 12 to 14 minutes for medium-rare or to desired doneness, turning once. *Makes 4 to 6 servings*

*Recipe for spice mix makes 1¼ cups. Store leftover spice mix in covered container in cool, dry place. Use with beef, pork or chicken.

Zesty Peppered Steak

Teriyaki Glazed Beef Kabobs

1¼ to 1½ pounds beef top or bottom sirloin, cut into 1-inch cubes
½ cup bottled teriyaki sauce
1 teaspoon Oriental sesame oil (optional)
1 clove garlic, minced
8 to 12 green onions
1 or 2 plum tomatoes, cut into slices (optional)

Thread beef cubes on metal or bamboo skewers. (Soak bamboo skewers in water for at least 20 minutes to keep them from burning.) Combine teriyaki sauce, sesame oil and garlic in small bowl. Brush beef and onions with part of glaze, saving some for grilling; let stand 15 to 30 minutes.

Oil hot grid to help prevent sticking. Grill beef, on covered grill, over medium KINGSFORD® Briquets, 6 to 9 minutes for medium doneness, turning several times and brushing with glaze. Add onions and tomatoes, if desired, to grid 3 to 4 minutes after beef; grill until onions and tomatoes are tender. Remove from grill; brush skewers, onions and tomatoes with remaining glaze.

Makes 4 servings

Fajita Kabobs

½ cup A.1.® Steak Sauce
½ cup mild, medium or hot thick and chunky salsa
1 (1½-pound) beef top round steak, cut into thin strips
2 large red onions, cut into wedges
2 large green bell peppers, cut into ¾-inch-wide strips
12 (6½-inch) flour tortillas, warmed
Dairy sour cream

In small bowl, blend steak sauce and salsa. Place steak strips in nonmetal bowl; coat with ½ cup salsa mixture. Cover; chill 1 hour, stirring occasionally.

Remove steak from marinade. Alternately thread steak, onions and peppers onto 6 (10-inch) metal skewers. Grill kabobs over medium heat for 10 to 15 minutes or until done, turning occasionally and brushing with remaining salsa mixture. Serve immediately with tortillas, sour cream and additional steak sauce.

Makes 6 servings

Teriyaki Glazed Beef Kabobs

Ratatouille Smothered Steak

1 cup chopped eggplant
1 cup chopped yellow and/or
   green bell peppers
1 clove garlic, minced
2 tablespoons olive oil
1 cup chopped fresh tomatoes
½ cup A.1.® Thick & Hearty
   Steak Sauce
½ teaspoon dried basil leaves
1 (1-pound) beef top round
   steak, about ¾ inch thick
   Additional A.1.® Thick &
   Hearty Steak Sauce,
   optional

In large skillet, over medium heat, sauté eggplant, peppers and garlic in oil until tender, about 5 minutes. Stir in tomatoes, steak sauce and basil; heat to a boil. Reduce heat; simmer 5 minutes. Keep warm.

Grill steak over medium heat or broil 6 inches from heat source 6 minutes on each side or to desired doneness, basting with additional steak sauce if desired. Slice steak; serve with warm sauce. Garnish as desired.   *Makes 4 servings*

Hot Off The Grill

The cooking rack, or grid, should be kept clean and free from any bits of charred food. Scrub the grid with a stiff wire brush while it is still warm.

Ratatouille Smothered Steak

Marinated Flank Steak with Pineapple

**1 can (15¼ ounces) DEL
  MONTE® Sliced Pineapple
  In Its Own Juice,
  undrained**
¼ cup teriyaki sauce
2 tablespoons honey
1 pound flank steak

1. Drain pineapple, reserving 2 tablespoons juice. Set aside pineapple for later use.

2. Combine reserved juice, teriyaki sauce and honey in shallow 2-quart dish; mix well. Add meat; turn to coat. Cover and refrigerate at least 30 minutes or overnight.

3. Remove meat from marinade, reserving marinade. Grill meat over hot coals (or broil), brushing occasionally with reserved marinade. Cook about 4 minutes on each side for rare; about 5 minutes on each side for medium; or about 6 minutes on each side for well done. During last 4 minutes of cooking, brush pineapple slices with marinade; grill until heated through.

4. Slice meat across grain; serve with pineapple. Garnish, if desired.

Makes 4 servings

Note: Marinade that has come into contact with raw meat must be discarded or boiled for several minutes before serving with cooked food.

Prep and Marinate Time: *35 minutes*
Cook Time: *10 minutes*

Marinated Flank Steak with Pineapple

Charcoal Beef Kabobs

½ cup vegetable oil
¼ cup lemon juice
1½ tablespoons (½ package)
  HIDDEN VALLEY® Salad
  Dressing Mix
2 pounds beef top round or
  boneless sirloin steak, cut
  into 1-inch cubes
1 or 2 red, yellow or green bell
  peppers, cut into 1-inch
  squares
16 pearl onions or 1 medium
  onion, cut into wedges
8 cherry tomatoes

Combine oil, lemon juice and dry salad dressing mix. Pour over beef cubes in shallow dish. Cover and refrigerate 1 hour or longer. Drain beef; reserve marinade. Thread beef cubes, peppers and onions onto skewers. Grill kabobs, on uncovered grill, over medium-hot KINGSFORD® Briquets 15 minutes, brushing often with reserved marinade and turning to brown all sides. A few minutes before serving, add cherry tomatoes to ends of skewers.

Makes 6 servings

Rosemary-Crusted Leg of Lamb

¼ cup Dijon mustard
2 large cloves garlic, minced
1 boneless butterflied leg of
  lamb (sirloin half, about
  2½ pounds), well trimmed
3 tablespoons chopped fresh
  rosemary leaves *or* 1
  tablespoon dried
  rosemary leaves, crushed
Fresh rosemary sprigs
  (optional)
Mint jelly (optional)

1. Prepare barbecue grill for direct cooking.

2. Combine mustard and garlic in small bowl; spread half of mixture with fingers or spatula over one side of lamb. Sprinkle with half of chopped rosemary; pat into mustard mixture. Turn lamb over; repeat with remaining mustard mixture and rosemary. Insert meat thermometer into center of thickest part of lamb.

3. Place lamb on grid. Grill, on covered grill, over medium coals 35 to 40 minutes or until thermometer registers 160°F for medium or until desired doneness, turning every 10 minutes.

4. Meanwhile, soak rosemary sprigs in water. Place rosemary sprigs directly on coals during last 10 minutes of grilling.

5. Transfer lamb to carving board; tent with foil. Let stand 10 minutes before carving into thin slices. Serve with mint jelly.

Makes 8 servings

Rosemary-Crusted Leg of Lamb

Barbecued Leg of Lamb

⅓ cup **A.1.® Steak Sauce**
2 tablespoons **red wine vinegar**
2 tablespoons **vegetable oil**
1 teaspoon **chili powder**
1 teaspoon **dried oregano leaves**
½ teaspoon **coarsely ground black pepper**
½ teaspoon **ground cinnamon**
2 cloves **garlic, crushed**
1 **(5- to 6-pound) leg of lamb, boned, butterflied and trimmed of fat (about 3 pounds after boning)**

In small bowl, combine steak sauce, vinegar, oil, chili powder, oregano, pepper, cinnamon and garlic. Place lamb in nonmetal dish; coat with steak sauce mixture. Cover; chill 1 hour, turning occasionally.

Remove lamb from marinade. Grill over medium heat 25 to 35 minutes or until done, turning often. Cut lamb into thin slices; serve hot.

Makes 12 servings

Lemon Pepper Lamb Kabobs

1½ cups **LAWRY'S® Lemon Pepper Marinade with Lemon Juice, divided**
1½ pounds **boneless lamb loin roast, cut into 1½-inch cubes**
12 **mushrooms**
2 **green bell peppers, cut into chunks**
2 **onions, cut into wedges**
Skewers

In large resealable plastic food storage bag, combine 1 cup Lemon Pepper Marinade and lamb; seal bag. Marinate in refrigerator at least 30 minutes. Remove lamb; discard used marinade. Alternately thread lamb and vegetables onto skewers. Grill or broil skewers 8 to 10 minutes or until desired doneness, turning once and basting often with additional ½ cup Lemon Pepper Marinade. *Do not baste during last 5 minutes of cooking.* Discard any remaining marinade.

Makes 6 servings

Serving Suggestion: Serve over a bed of couscous with a Greek salad.

Palamidis Lamb Kabobs

1½ pounds ground lamb or
    ground beef
1 small eggplant (about ¾
    pound), unpeeled and
    finely chopped
1⅓ cups FRENCH'S® French
    Fried Onions
1 egg, beaten
½ cup plain dry bread crumbs
¼ cup FRENCH'S®
    Worcestershire Sauce
2 teaspoons Italian seasoning
1 teaspoon salt
¼ teaspoon ground black
    pepper

Combine lamb, eggplant, French Fried Onions, egg, bread crumbs, Worcestershire, Italian seasoning, salt and pepper in large bowl. Shape mixture into 2-inch meatballs, pressing firmly.

Thread meatballs onto metal skewers. Place skewers on oiled grid. Grill over medium-high coals 15 minutes or until lamb is no longer pink, carefully turning skewers occasionally. *Makes 6 servings*

Tip: To prevent meat from sticking to hands, occasionally wet hands with cold water.

Prep Time: 20 minutes
Cook Time: 15 minutes

Lamb Chops with Fresh Herbs

⅓ cup red wine vinegar
⅓ cup vegetable oil
2 tablespoons soy sauce
2 tablespoons sherry
1 tablespoon lemon juice
1 tablespoon **LAWRY'S®** Seasoned Salt
1 teaspoon **LAWRY'S® Garlic** Powder with Parsley
1 teaspoon chopped fresh oregano
1 teaspoon chopped fresh rosemary
1 teaspoon chopped fresh thyme
1 teaspoon chopped fresh marjoram
1 teaspoon dry mustard
½ teaspoon white pepper
8 lamb loin chops (about 2 pounds), cut 1 inch thick

In large resealable plastic food storage bag, combine all ingredients except chops; mix well. Remove ½ cup marinade for basting. Add chops; seal bag. Marinate in refrigerator at least 1 hour. Remove chops; discard used marinade. Grill or broil chops 8 minutes or until desired doneness, turning once and basting often with additional ½ cup marinade. *Do not baste during last 5 minutes of cooking.* Discard any remaining marinade.   *Makes 4 to 6 servings*

Serving Suggestion: Serve with mashed potatoes and fresh green beans.

Hint: Substitute ¼ to ½ teaspoon dried herbs for each teaspoon of fresh herbs.

Hot Off The Grill

Watch foods carefully during grilling. Set a timer to remind you when it's time to check the food on the grill.

Lamb Chops with Fresh Herbs

Mint Marinated Racks of Lamb

2 whole racks (6 ribs each)
    loin lamb chops (about
    3 pounds), well trimmed
1 cup dry red wine
½ cup chopped fresh mint
    leaves (optional)
3 cloves garlic, minced
¼ cup Dijon mustard
2 tablespoons chopped fresh
    mint leaves *or* 2 teaspoons
    dried mint leaves, crushed
⅔ cup dry bread crumbs

Place lamb in large resealable plastic food storage bag. Combine wine, ½ cup mint and garlic in small bowl. Pour over chops. Seal bag tightly; turn to coat. Marinate in refrigerator at least 2 hours or up to 4 hours, turning occasionally.

Prepare grill. Drain lamb, discarding marinade. Pat lamb dry with paper towels. Place lamb in shallow glass dish or on cutting board. Combine mustard and 2 tablespoons mint in small bowl; spread over meaty side of lamb. Pat bread crumbs evenly over mustard mixture. Place lamb, crumb side down, on grid. Grill, on covered grill, over medium coals 10 minutes. Carefully turn; continue to grill, covered, 20 to 22 minutes more for medium or to desired doneness. Place lamb on carving board. Slice between ribs into individual chops.

Makes 4 servings

Teriyaki Butterflied Lamb

¾ cup KIKKOMAN® Teriyaki
    Baste & Glaze
1 teaspoon grated orange
    peel
1 tablespoon orange juice
1 teaspoon TABASCO® brand
    Pepper Sauce
4 cloves garlic, pressed
1 (4-pound) lamb leg, sirloin
    or shank half, boned and
    butterflied

Combine teriyaki baste & glaze, orange peel, orange juice, TABASCO® Sauce and garlic; set aside. Trim and discard "fell" and excess fat from lamb. Place lamb on grill 5 inches from hot coals; brush lightly with baste & glaze mixture. Cook 40 minutes, or until meat thermometer inserted into thickest part registers 140°F (for rare), or to desired doneness, turning lamb over occasionally and brushing frequently with remaining baste & glaze mixture. (Or, place lamb on rack of broiler pan. Broil 5 inches from heat 20 minutes, brushing occasionally with baste & glaze mixture. Turn lamb over. Broil 20 minutes longer, or until meat thermometer inserted into thickest part registers 140°F [for rare], or to desired doneness, brushing occasionally with remaining baste & glaze mixture.)

Makes 6 to 8 servings

Mint Marinated Rack of Lamb

Grilled Lamb and Cracked Bulgur Wheat

1½ pounds boneless lamb steaks, sliced ¼ inch thick
½ cup chopped fresh mint*
¼ cup FILIPPO BERIO® Extra Virgin Olive Oil
2 tablespoons lemon juice
1 large clove garlic, minced
1½ teaspoons chopped fresh parsley
1½ teaspoons chopped shallot
Salt and freshly ground black pepper
Cracked Bulgur Wheat (recipe follows)
Grilled vegetables, fresh herb sprigs and pita bread (optional)

Omit mint if fresh is unavailable. Do not substitute dried mint leaves.

Place lamb in single layer in large shallow glass dish. In medium bowl, whisk together mint, olive oil, lemon juice, garlic, parsley and shallot. Pour marinade over lamb; turn to coat both sides. Cover; marinate in refrigerator 2 to 4 hours, turning occasionally. Remove lamb; discard marinade.

Brush barbecue grid with olive oil. Grill lamb, on covered grill, over hot coals 1 to 2 minutes per side or until desired doneness is reached. Or, broil lamb, 4 to 5 inches from heat, 1 to 2 minutes per side or until desired doneness is reached. (Do not overcook lamb). Season to taste with salt and pepper. Cut each steak into 3 to 4 pieces. To serve, place portion of Cracked Bulgur Wheat in center of 6 serving plates. Surround with 3 to 4 pieces of lamb. Garnish with vegetables, herbs and pita bread, if desired.

Makes 6 servings

Cracked Bulgur Wheat

1 tablespoon FILIPPO BERIO® Olive Oil
1 large onion, chopped
2 large cloves garlic, minced
4 cups cracked bulgur wheat
2 cups chicken broth, defatted
2 cups water
1 tablespoon chopped fresh rosemary*
2 teaspoons chopped fresh sage*
Salt and freshly ground black pepper

Omit herbs if fresh are unavailable. Do not substitute dried herb leaves.

In large saucepan, heat olive oil over low heat until hot. Add onion and garlic; cook and stir 5 minutes or until onion is softened but not browned. Add bulgur; stir until coated. Add chicken broth, water, rosemary and sage. Bring to a boil over high heat. Remove from heat. Cover; let stand 20 to 30 minutes or until liquid is absorbed. Season to taste with salt and pepper.

Makes 6 to 8 servings

Calypso Pork Chop

1 ripe medium papaya, peeled, halved lengthwise and seeded
1 teaspoon paprika
½ teaspoon dried thyme leaves
¼ teaspoon salt
¼ teaspoon ground allspice
4 center-cut pork loin chops (about 1½ pounds), cut ¾ inch thick
5 tablespoons fresh lime juice, divided
2 tablespoons plus 1½ teaspoons seeded, chopped jalapeño peppers,* divided
1 tablespoon vegetable oil
1½ teaspoons grated fresh ginger, divided
1 teaspoon sugar
¼ cup finely diced red bell pepper
Additional chopped jalapeño pepper for garnish

*Jalapeño peppers can sting and irritate the skin; wear rubber gloves when handling peppers and do not touch eyes. Wash your hands after handling peppers.

1. Chop papaya flesh into ¼-inch pieces. Chop enough papaya to measure 1½ cups; set aside.

2. Combine paprika, thyme, salt and allspice in small bowl; rub over both sides of pork chops with fingers. Place chops in large resealable plastic food storage bag.

3. Combine 3 tablespoons lime juice, 2 tablespoons jalapeños, oil, 1 teaspoon ginger and sugar in small bowl; pour over chops. Seal bag tightly, turning to coat. Marinate in refrigerator 1 to 2 hours.

4. Combine papaya, bell pepper, remaining 2 tablespoons lime juice, remaining 1½ teaspoons jalapeños and remaining ½ teaspoon ginger in another small bowl; cover and refrigerate until serving.

5. Prepare barbecue grill for direct cooking.

6. Meanwhile, drain chops; discard marinade. Place chops on grid. Grill chops, on covered grill, over medium coals 10 to 12 minutes or until pork is juicy and barely pink in center, turning halfway through grilling time. Serve chops topped with papaya mixture. Garnish, if desired.   *Makes 4 servings*

Calypso Pork Chop

Grilled Pork Tenderloin with Apple Salsa

1 tablespoon chili powder
½ teaspoon garlic powder
1 pound pork tenderloin
2 Granny Smith apples, peeled, cored and finely chopped
1 can (4 ounces) chopped green chilies
¼ cup lemon juice
3 tablespoons finely chopped fresh cilantro
1 clove garlic, minced
1 teaspoon dried oregano leaves, crushed
½ teaspoon salt

1. Spray grid well with nonstick cooking spray. Preheat grill to medium-high heat.

2. Combine chili powder and garlic powder in small bowl; mix well. Coat pork with spice mixture.

3. Grill pork 30 minutes, turning occasionally, until internal temperature reaches 155°F when tested with meat thermometer in thickest part of tenderloin. Cover with foil and let rest 10 minutes before slicing.

4. To make apple salsa, combine apples, chilies, lemon juice, cilantro, garlic, oregano and salt in medium bowl; mix well.

5. Slice pork across grain; serve with salsa. Garnish, if desired.

Makes 4 servings

Mustard-Glazed Ribs

¾ cup beer
½ cup firmly packed dark brown sugar
½ cup spicy brown mustard
3 tablespoons soy sauce
1 tablespoon catsup
¾ teaspoon **TABASCO®** brand Pepper Sauce
½ teaspoon ground cloves
4 pounds pork spareribs or beef baby back ribs

In medium bowl, combine beer, sugar, mustard, soy sauce, catsup, TABASCO® Sauce and cloves; mix well. Position grill rack as far from coals as possible. Place ribs on grill over low heat. For pork ribs, grill 45 minutes; turn occasionally. Brush with mustard glaze. Grill 30 minutes longer or until meat is cooked through; turn and baste ribs often with mustard glaze. (For beef baby back ribs, grill 15 minutes. Brush with mustard glaze. Grill 30 minutes longer or until meat is cooked to desired doneness; turn and baste ribs often with mustard glaze.) Heat any remaining glaze to a boil; serve with ribs.

Makes 4 servings

Grilled Pork Tenderloin with Apple Salsa

Herb and Orange Pork Chops

2 cups orange juice
3 tablespoons vegetable oil,
 divided
1½ teaspoons LAWRY'S®
 Seasoned Salt
1½ teaspoons LAWRY'S®
 Lemon Pepper
1½ teaspoons LAWRY'S® Garlic
 Powder with Parsley
1 teaspoon dried basil,
 crushed
½ teaspoon dried rosemary,
 crushed
4 pork loin chops, cut ½ inch
 thick
½ cup thinly sliced green
 onions
1 teaspoon grated fresh
 orange peel

In medium bowl, combine orange juice, 2 tablespoons oil and next 5 ingredients; mix well. In large resealable plastic food storage bag, combine 1 cup marinade and chops; seal bag. Marinate in refrigerator at least 1 hour. Remove chops; discard used marinade. Grill or broil chops 8 to 10 minutes or until no longer pink in center, turning halfway through grilling time. In large skillet, heat 1 tablespoon oil; add onions and orange peel and cook over medium heat 1 minute. Add additional marinade; reduce heat to low and cook until reduced by half. Serve over chops.

Makes 4 servings

Serving Suggestion: Serve with fresh fruit.

Hot Off The Grill

Top and bottom vents should be open before starting a charcoal grill. Close vents when cooking is finished to extinguish the coals.

Herb and Orange Pork Chops

Jamaican Jerked Pork

1½ cups orange juice
1 medium onion, diced
1 jalapeño pepper, seeded and minced*
2 cloves garlic, minced
2 tablespoons brown sugar
1 tablespoon olive oil
1½ teaspoons dried thyme leaves
1 teaspoon salt
1 teaspoon black pepper
½ teaspoon ground allspice
¼ teaspoon ground nutmeg
1½ pounds boneless pork shoulder, trimmed

Chili peppers can sting and irritate the skin; wear rubber gloves when handling peppers and do not touch eyes.

Combine all ingredients, except pork, in medium bowl; mix well.

Pierce pork a few times with fork. Place in large resealable plastic food storage bag. Pour orange juice mixture into bag. Close bag securely, turning to coat. Marinate in refrigerator overnight, turning occasionally.

Prepare grill for direct cooking. Drain pork; reserve marinade.

Place pork on grid. Grill, covered, over medium-high heat 45 to 60 minutes or until internal temperature reaches 155°F when tested with meat thermometer inserted into thickest part of pork, turning occasionally. Remove from grill; let stand on cutting board 5 minutes.

Meanwhile, pour reserved marinade into large saucepan. Bring to a boil over high heat. Cover, reduce to a simmer and cook 20 minutes or until onions are soft.

Slice or "hack" pork into bite-size pieces. Add pork to saucepan with cooking marinade. Bring to a simmer. Simmer, uncovered, 15 minutes.

Makes 4 servings

Grilled Spiced Pork Tenderloin

1 whole pork tenderloin (1¼ pounds)
2 tablespoons lemon juice
1 tablespoon FILIPPO BERIO® Olive Oil
2 cloves garlic, minced
½ teaspoon ground coriander
½ teaspoon ground cumin
½ teaspoon chili powder

Place tenderloin in shallow glass dish. In small bowl, combine lemon juice, olive oil, garlic, coriander, cumin and chili powder. Spread olive oil mixture over all sides of tenderloin. Cover; marinate in refrigerator at least 2 hours or overnight, turning once. Remove tenderloin, reserving marinade.

Brush barbecue grid with olive oil. Grill tenderloin, on covered grill, over hot coals 25 to 30 minutes, turning and brushing with reserved marinade halfway through grilling time, or until tenderloin is juicy and barely pink in center.

Makes 3 to 4 servings

Jamaican Jerked Pork

Garlic-Pepper Skewered Pork

1 boneless pork loin roast
   (about 2½ pounds)
6 to 15 cloves garlic, minced
⅓ cup lime juice
3 tablespoons firmly packed
   brown sugar
3 tablespoons soy sauce
2 tablespoons vegetable oil
2 teaspoons black pepper
¼ teaspoon cayenne pepper
8 green onions, cut into 2-inch
   pieces (optional)

Cut pork crosswise into six ½-inch-thick chops, reserving remaining roast. (Each chop may separate into 2 pieces.) Set chops aside in 13×9×2-inch glass dish. Cut remaining pork roast lengthwise into 2 pieces. Cut each piece into ⅛-inch-thick strips; place in dish with chops. To prepare marinade, combine all remaining ingredients except green onions in small bowl. Pour marinade over pork chops and slices; cover and refrigerate at least 1 hour or overnight. Thread pork slices ribbon style onto metal skewers, alternating pork with green onions. Grill skewered pork slices and chops over medium-hot KINGSFORD® Briquets about 3 minutes per side until no longer pink in center. (Chops may require 1 to 2 minutes longer.) *Do not overcook.* Serve skewered pork immediately.   *Makes 4 to 6 servings*

Apricot-Glazed Ham Steaks

½ cup A.1.® Bold & Spicy Steak
   Sauce
⅓ cup apricot preserves
¼ cup firmly packed light
   brown sugar
¼ cup orange juice
2 (1-pound) fully cooked
   center-cut ham slices,
   ½ inch thick
Orange slices and chopped
   parsley, for garnish

In small bowl, combine steak sauce, apricot preserves, brown sugar and orange juice. Reserve ½ cup glaze.

In small saucepan, over medium heat, heat remaining glaze to a boil; keep warm.

Grill ham steaks over medium heat 3 to 4 minutes on each side or until heated through, basting with reserved glaze. To serve, drizzle warm glaze over ham steaks; garnish with orange slices and parsley if desired.   *Makes 6 to 8 servings*

Garlic-Pepper Skewered Pork

Pork Chops with Apple-Sage Stuffing

**6 center-cut pork chops
(3 pounds), about 1 inch
thick**
¾ cup dry vermouth, divided
**4 tablespoons minced fresh
sage *or* 4 teaspoons
rubbed sage, divided**
2 tablespoons soy sauce
1 tablespoon olive oil
2 cloves garlic, minced
**½ teaspoon black pepper,
divided**
1 tablespoon butter
1 medium onion, diced
1 apple, cored and diced
½ teaspoon salt
**2 cups fresh firm-textured
white bread crumbs**
Curly endive
Plum slices

Cut pocket in each chop using tip of thin, sharp knife. Combine ¼ cup vermouth, 2 tablespoons fresh sage (or 2 teaspoons rubbed sage), soy sauce, oil, garlic and ¼ teaspoon pepper in glass dish; add pork chops, turning to coat. Heat butter in large skillet over medium heat until foamy. Add onion and apple; cook and stir about 6 minutes until onion is tender. Stir in remaining ½ cup vermouth, 2 tablespoons sage, ¼ teaspoon pepper and salt. Cook and stir over high heat about 3 minutes until liquid is almost gone. Transfer onion mixture to large bowl. Stir in bread crumbs.

Remove pork chops from marinade; discard marinade. Spoon onion mixture into pockets of pork chops. Close openings with wooden picks. (Soak wooden picks in hot water 15 minutes to prevent burning.) Grill pork chops on covered grill over medium KINGSFORD® Briquets about 5 minutes per side until barely pink in center. Garnish with endive and plum slices.

Makes 6 servings

Hot Off The Grill

A few wonderful apple varieties to try in this stuffing include Cortland apples and Granny Smith apples. Both will give you a slightly different flavor and color. The Cortland apples have a sweet-tart flavor and are shiny red; Granny Smith apples have a tart flavor and are yellow to green.

Pork Chop with Apple-Sage Stuffing

Pork Tenderloin with Grilled Apple Cream Sauce

1 can (6 ounces) frozen apple juice concentrate, thawed and divided (¾ cup)
½ cup Calvados or brandy, divided
2 tablespoons Dijon mustard
1 tablespoon olive oil
3 cloves garlic, minced
1¼ teaspoons salt, divided
¼ teaspoon black pepper
1½ pounds pork tenderloin
2 green or red apples, cored
1 tablespoon butter
½ large red onion, cut into thin slivers
½ cup heavy cream
Fresh thyme sprigs

Reserve 2 tablespoons juice concentrate. Combine remaining juice concentrate, ¼ cup Calvados, mustard, oil, garlic, 1 teaspoon salt and pepper in glass dish. Add pork; turn to coat. Cover and refrigerate 2 hours, turning pork occasionally. Cut apples crosswise into ⅜-inch rings. Remove pork from marinade; discard marinade. Grill pork on covered grill over medium KINGSFORD® Briquets about 20 minutes, turning 3 times, until meat thermometer inserted in thickest part registers 155°F. Grill apples about 4 minutes per side until tender; cut rings into quarters. Melt butter in large skillet over medium heat. Add onion; cook and stir until soft. Stir in apples, remaining ¼ cup Calvados, ¼ teaspoon salt and reserved 2 tablespoons apple juice. Add cream; heat through. Cut pork crosswise into ½-inch slices; spoon sauce over pork. Garnish with fresh thyme. *Makes 4 servings*

Hot Off The Grill

Serve this mouthwatering recipe with a tossed green salad and baked acorn squash for a delicious hearty fall meal.

Pork Tenderloin with Grilled Apple Cream Sauce

Pork Chops with Orange-Radish Relish

2 cups orange juice
⅓ cup lime juice
⅓ cup packed brown sugar
3 medium oranges, peeled,
**   seeded and cut into**
**   ¼-inch pieces**
¼ cup chopped red onion
¼ cup diced radishes
2 tablespoons finely chopped
**   fresh cilantro**
6 pork chops (¾ inch thick)
**   Salt and black pepper**
**   Orange curls and radishes**

Combine both juices and brown sugar in saucepan. Cook mixture at a low boil, stirring often, about 20 minutes until reduced to about ½ cup and it has a syruplike consistency. Set aside ¼ cup sauce for basting.

Meanwhile, prepare Orange-Radish Relish by combining oranges, onion and diced radishes in colander or strainer and drain well; transfer to bowl. Add cilantro and gently stir in remaining orange syrup. Season pork with salt and pepper.

Oil hot grid to help prevent sticking. Grill pork, on covered grill, over medium KINGSFORD® Briquets, 7 to 10 minutes. (Pork is done at 160°F; it should be juicy and slightly pink in center.) Halfway through cooking, brush with reserved ¼ cup orange syrup and turn once. Serve with Orange-Radish Relish. Garnish with orange curls and radishes.   *Makes 6 servings*

Cranberry Glazed Pork Tenderloin

1 cup whole berry cranberry
**   sauce**
⅓ cup A.1.® Steak Sauce
¼ cup chopped green onions
2 tablespoons reduced sodium
**   soy sauce**
2 tablespoons firmly packed
**   light brown sugar**
1 teaspoon grated fresh
**   ginger**
1 (1-pound) pork tenderloin

In small saucepan, combine cranberry sauce, steak sauce, onions, soy sauce, brown sugar and ginger. Over medium heat, cook until mixture is blended and heated through. Remove ⅓ cup sauce; cool. Keep remaining sauce warm.

Grill pork over medium heat 20 to 30 minutes or until done, turning and brushing occasionally with ⅓ cup reserved sauce. Serve hot with warm sauce.   *Makes 4 servings*

Pork Chop with Orange-Radish Relish

Memphis Pork Ribs

1 tablespoon chili powder
1 tablespoon dried parsley
2 teaspoons onion powder
2 teaspoons garlic powder
2 teaspoons dried oregano
    leaves
2 teaspoons paprika
2 teaspoons black pepper
1½ teaspoons salt
4 pounds pork spareribs, cut
    into 4 racks
    Tennessee **BBQ** Sauce
    (recipe follows)

Combine chili powder, parsley, onion powder, garlic powder, oregano, paprika, pepper and salt in small bowl; mix well.

Rub spice mixture onto ribs. Cover; marinate in refrigerator at least 2 hours or overnight.

Preheat oven to 350°F. Place ribs in foil-lined shallow roasting pan. Bake 30 minutes.

Meanwhile, prepare grill for direct cooking. Prepare Tennessee BBQ sauce.

Place ribs on grid. Grill, covered, over medium heat 10 minutes. Brush with sauce. Continue grilling 10 minutes or until ribs are tender, brushing with sauce occasionally. Serve any remaining sauce on the side for dipping. *Makes 4 servings*

Tennessee BBQ Sauce

3 cups prepared barbecue sauce
¼ cup cider vinegar
¼ cup honey
2 teaspoons onion powder
2 teaspoons garlic powder
  Dash hot pepper sauce

Combine all ingredients in medium bowl; mix well.

Makes about 3½ cups

Memphis Pork Ribs

Kickin' Chicken & Turkey

Smoked Barbecued Turkey (page 286)

Southwest Chicken (page 258)

Grilled Chicken Breasts with Tropical Salsa

1 package BUTTERBALL® Skinless Boneless Chicken Breast Fillets
1 cup cubed mango
1 kiwi, diced
2 green onions, chopped
2 tablespoons chopped fresh cilantro
1 tablespoon fresh lime juice
½ teaspoon red pepper flakes

Grill chicken fillets 4 to 5 minutes on each side or until internal temperature reaches 170°F and no longer pink in center. Combine mango, kiwi, onions, cilantro, lime juice and red pepper flakes in medium bowl. Serve with chicken.

Serves 4

Preparation Time: *20 minutes*

Black Bean Garnachas

1 can (14½ ounces)
    DEL MONTE® Diced
    Tomatoes with Garlic &
    Onion
1 can (15 ounces) black or
    pinto beans, drained
2 cloves garlic, minced
1 to 2 teaspoons minced
    jalapeño peppers
    (optional)
½ teaspoon ground cumin
1 cup cubed grilled chicken
4 flour tortillas
½ cup (2 ounces) shredded
    sharp Cheddar cheese

1. Combine undrained tomatoes, beans, garlic, jalapeño peppers and cumin in large skillet. Cook over medium-high heat 5 to 7 minutes or until thickened, stirring occasionally. Stir in chicken. Season with salt and pepper, if desired.

2. Arrange tortillas in single layer on grill over medium coals. Spread about ¾ cup chicken mixture over each tortilla. Top with cheese.

3. Cook about 3 minutes or until bottoms of tortillas are browned and cheese is melted. Top with shredded lettuce, diced avocado and sliced jalapeño peppers, if desired.

Makes 4 servings

Variation: Prepare chicken mixture as directed above. Place a tortilla in a dry skillet over medium heat. Spread with about ¾ cup chicken mixture; top with 2 tablespoons cheese. Cover and cook about 3 minutes or until bottom of tortilla is browned and cheese is melted. Repeat with remaining tortillas.

Prep Time: *5 minutes*
Cook Time: *10 minutes*

Black Bean Garnacha

Blue Cheese Stuffed Chicken Breasts

2 tablespoons margarine or butter, softened, divided
½ cup (2 ounces) crumbled blue cheese
¾ teaspoon dried thyme leaves
2 whole boneless chicken breasts with skin (not split)
1 tablespoon bottled or fresh lemon juice
½ teaspoon paprika

1. Prepare grill for grilling. Combine 1 tablespoon margarine, blue cheese and thyme in small bowl until blended. Season with salt and pepper.

2. Loosen skin over breast of chicken by pushing fingers between skin and meat, taking care not to tear skin. Spread blue cheese mixture under skin with a rubber spatula or small spoon; massage skin to evenly spread cheese mixture.

3. Place chicken, skin side down, on grid over medium coals. Grill over covered grill 5 minutes. Meanwhile, melt remaining 1 tablespoon margarine; stir in lemon juice and paprika. Turn chicken; brush with lemon juice mixture. Grill 5 to 7 minutes more or until chicken is cooked through. Transfer chicken to carving board; cut each breast in half.   *Makes 4 servings*

Serving Suggestion: Serve with steamed new potatoes and broccoli.

Prep and Cook Time: *22 minutes*

Tandoori-Style Chicken

½ cup plain regular or lowfat yogurt
¼ cup A.1.® Steak Sauce
¼ cup chopped fresh mint
1 teaspoon paprika
½ teaspoon ground red pepper
3 cloves garlic, crushed
1 (2½- to 3-pound) chicken, cut into 4 pieces
Raita (recipe follows)

In small bowl, combine yogurt, steak sauce, mint, paprika, red pepper and garlic. Place chicken pieces in glass dish; coat with yogurt mixture. Cover; chill 1 hour, turning occasionally.

Remove chicken from marinade. Grill chicken over medium heat 30 to 35 minutes or until done, turning occasionally. Serve with Raita.   *Makes 4 servings*

Raita: In small bowl, combine ½ cup plain regular or lowfat yogurt; ½ cup finely diced seeded peeled cucumber; 1 tablespoon A.1.® Steak Sauce; 1 tablespoon finely chopped fresh mint and 2 teaspoons honey. Cover; chill until serving time.

Blue Cheese Stuffed Chicken Breast

Hot, Spicy, Tangy, Sticky Chicken

1 chicken (3½ to 4 pounds),
    cut up
1 cup cider vinegar
1 tablespoon Worcestershire
    sauce
1 tablespoon chili powder
1 teaspoon salt
1 teaspoon black pepper
1 teaspoon hot pepper sauce
¾ cup **K.C. MASTERPIECE**®
    Barbecue Sauce

Place chicken in a shallow glass dish or large heavy plastic bag. Combine vinegar, Worcestershire sauce, chili powder, salt, pepper and hot pepper sauce in small bowl; pour over chicken pieces. Cover dish or seal bag. Marinate in refrigerator at least 4 hours, turning several times.

Oil hot grid to help prevent sticking. Place dark meat pieces on grill 10 minutes before white meat pieces (dark meat takes longer to cook). Grill chicken on covered grill, over medium KINGSFORD® Briquets, 30 to 45 minutes, turning once or twice. Turn and baste with K.C. Masterpiece® Barbecue Sauce last 10 minutes of cooking. Remove chicken from grill; baste with barbecue sauce. Chicken is done when meat is no longer pink by bone. *Makes 4 servings*

Spicy Thai Chicken

¾ cup canned cream of
    coconut
3 tablespoons lime juice
3 tablespoons soy sauce
3 large green onions, cut up
3 large cloves garlic
8 sprigs cilantro
3 anchovy filets
1 teaspoon **TABASCO**® brand
    Pepper Sauce
2 whole boneless skinless
    chicken breasts, cut in half
    (about 1½ pounds)

In container of blender or food processor, combine cream of coconut, lime juice, soy sauce, green onions, garlic, cilantro, anchovies and TABASCO® Sauce. Cover; blend until smooth. Place chicken in large shallow dish or plastic bag; add marinade. Cover; refrigerate at least 2 hours, turning chicken occasionally.

Remove chicken from marinade; reserve marinade. Place chicken on grill about 5 inches from source of heat. Brush generously with marinade. Grill 5 minutes. Turn chicken; brush with marinade. Grill 5 minutes longer or until chicken is cooked. Heat any remaining marinade to a boil; boil 1 minute. Serve as a dipping sauce for chicken. *Makes 4 servings*

Hot, Spicy, Tangy, Sticky Chicken

Buffalo Chicken Drumsticks

8 large chicken drumsticks
(about 2 pounds)
3 tablespoons hot pepper
sauce
1 tablespoon vegetable oil
1 clove garlic, minced
¼ cup mayonnaise
3 tablespoons sour cream
1½ tablespoons white wine
vinegar
¼ teaspoon sugar
⅓ cup (1½ ounces) crumbled
Roquefort or blue cheese
2 cups hickory chips
Celery sticks

Place chicken in large resealable plastic food storage bag. Combine pepper sauce, oil and garlic in small bowl; pour over chicken. Seal bag tightly; turn to coat. Marinate in refrigerator at least 1 hour or, for hotter flavor, up to 24 hours, turning occasionally.

For blue cheese dressing, combine mayonnaise, sour cream, vinegar and sugar in another small bowl. Stir in cheese; cover and refrigerate until serving.

Prepare grill. Meanwhile, cover hickory chips with cold water; soak 20 minutes. Drain chicken, discarding marinade. Drain hickory chips; sprinkle over coals. Place chicken on grid. Grill, on covered grill, over medium-hot coals 25 to 30 minutes or until chicken is tender when pierced with fork and no longer pink near bone, turning 3 to 4 times. Serve with blue cheese dressing and celery sticks.

Makes 4 servings

Hot Off The Grill

Do not crowd pieces of food on the grill. Food will cook more evenly with a ¾-inch space between pieces.

Buffalo Chicken Drumsticks

Chicken Ribbons Satay

½ cup creamy peanut butter
½ cup water
¼ cup soy sauce
4 cloves garlic, pressed
3 tablespoons lemon juice
2 tablespoons firmly packed
   brown sugar
¾ teaspoon ground ginger
½ teaspoon crushed red
   pepper flakes
4 boneless skinless chicken
   breast halves
   Sliced green onion tops for
   garnish

Combine peanut butter, water, soy sauce, garlic, lemon juice, brown sugar, ginger and red pepper flakes in a small saucepan. Cook over medium heat 1 minute or until smooth; cool. Remove garlic from sauce; discard. Reserve half of sauce for dipping. Cut chicken lengthwise into 1-inch-wide strips. Thread onto 8 metal or bamboo skewers. (Soak bamboo skewers in water at least 20 minutes to keep them from burning.)

Oil hot grid to help prevent sticking. Grill chicken, on a covered grill, over medium-hot KINGSFORD® Briquets, 6 to 8 minutes until chicken is no longer pink in center, turning once. Baste with sauce once or twice during cooking. Serve with reserved sauce garnished with sliced green onion.   *Makes 4 servings*

Grilled Lemon Minted Chicken Breasts

3 packages BUTTERBALL®
   Chicken Split Breasts
1 cup fresh lemon juice
¼ cup chopped fresh mint
   leaves
2 teaspoons grated lemon
   peel
½ teaspoon red pepper flakes

Combine lemon juice, mint leaves, lemon peel and red pepper flakes in small bowl. Grill chicken, bone side up, over hot coals 15 to 20 minutes, brushing frequently with lemon mixture. Turn and grill chicken 15 to 20 minutes longer or until internal temperature reaches 170°F and no longer pink in center. Serve grilled chicken with lemon minted couscous.*   *Serves 9*

To prepare lemon minted couscous, prepare couscous according to package directions. Add a squeeze of fresh lemon and chopped fresh mint.

Preparation Time: *30 to 40 minutes*

Chicken Ribbons Satay

Chicken with Mediterranean Salsa

¼ cup olive oil
3 tablespoons lemon juice
4 to 6 boneless skinless
    chicken breast halves
Salt and black pepper
Rosemary sprigs (optional)
Mediterranean Salsa (recipe
    follows)
Additional rosemary sprigs
    for garnish

Combine olive oil and lemon juice in a shallow glass dish; add chicken. Turn chicken breasts to lightly coat with mixture; let stand 10 to 15 minutes. Remove chicken from dish and wipe off excess oil; season with salt and pepper.

Oil hot grid to help prevent sticking. Place chicken on grid and place a sprig of rosemary on each chicken breast. Grill chicken, on a covered grill, over medium KINGSFORD® Briquets, 10 to 15 minutes until chicken is no longer pink in center, turning once or twice. Serve with Mediterranean Salsa. Garnish, if desired.

Makes 4 to 6 servings

Mediterranean Salsa

2 tablespoons olive oil
2 tablespoons white wine vinegar
1 clove garlic, minced
2 tablespoons finely chopped fresh basil *or* 1 teaspoon
    dried basil leaves, crushed
1 tablespoon finely chopped fresh rosemary *or* 1
    teaspoon dried rosemary, crushed
1 teaspoon sugar
¼ teaspoon black pepper
10 to 15 kalamata olives,* seeded and coarsely chopped
    or ⅓ cup coarsely chopped whole pitted ripe olives
½ cup chopped seeded cucumber
¼ cup finely chopped red onion
1 cup chopped seeded tomatoes (about ½ pound)
⅓ cup crumbled feta cheese

Kalamata olives are brine-cured Greek-style olives. They are available in large supermarkets.

Combine oil, vinegar, garlic, basil, rosemary, sugar and pepper in a medium bowl. Add olives, cucumber and onion; toss to coat. Cover and refrigerate until ready to serve. Just before serving, gently stir in tomatoes and feta cheese.

Makes about 2 cups

Chicken with Mediterranean Salsa

Grilled Chicken and Vegetable Kabobs

⅓ **cup olive oil**
¼ **cup lemon juice**
 4 **cloves garlic, coarsely**
    chopped
½ **teaspoon dried tarragon**
    leaves
½ **teaspoon salt**
½ **teaspoon lemon pepper**
 I **pound chicken tenders**
 6 **ounces mushrooms**
 I **cup sliced zucchini**
½ **cup cubed green bell pepper**
½ **cup cubed red bell pepper**
 I **red onion, quartered**
 6 **cherry tomatoes**
 3 **cups hot cooked rice**

Combine oil, lemon juice, garlic, tarragon, salt and lemon pepper in large resealable plastic food storage bag. Add chicken, mushrooms, zucchini, bell peppers, onion and tomatoes. Seal and shake until well coated. Refrigerate at least 8 hours, turning occasionally.

Soak 6 (10-inch) wooden skewers in water 30 minutes; set aside.

Remove chicken and vegetables from marinade; discard marinade. Thread chicken and vegetables onto skewers.

Coat grill grid with nonstick cooking spray; place skewers on grid. Grill covered over medium-hot coals 3 to 4 minutes on each side or until chicken is no longer pink in center.

Remove chicken and vegetables from skewers and serve over rice.

Makes 6 servings

Serving Suggestion: Serve with sliced fresh pineapple and green grapes.

Hot Off The Grill

For additional flavor, toss water-soaked wood chips, such as hickory or mesquite, onto hot coals before adding food. Adding wood chips to the coals will create smoke, so make sure the grill is in a well-ventilated area away from any open windows.

Grilled Chicken and Vegetable Kabob

Grilled Chicken Pasta Toss

1½ cups **LAWRY'S®** Herb &
Garlic Marinade with
Lemon Juice, divided
6 **boneless, skinless chicken
breast halves (about
1½ pounds)**
3 **tablespoons vegetable oil,
divided**
1½ **cups broccoli flowerettes
and sliced stems**
1 **cup Chinese pea pods**
1 **cup diagonally sliced carrots**
1 **can (2¼ ounces) sliced
pitted black olives,
drained**
8 **ounces fettuccine or
linguine noodles, cooked,
drained and kept hot**

In large resealable plastic food storage bag, combine 1 cup Herb & Garlic Marinade and chicken; seal bag. Marinate in refrigerator at least 30 minutes. Remove chicken; discard used marinade. Grill or broil chicken 10 to 15 minutes or until no longer pink in center and juices run clear when cut, turning once and basting often with additional ¼ cup Herb & Garlic Marinade. *Do not baste during last 5 minutes of cooking.* Discard any remaining marinade. Cut chicken into slices. In medium skillet, heat 2 tablespoons oil. Cook broccoli, pea pods and carrots over medium-high heat until crisp-tender. In large bowl, combine cooked vegetables, olives, hot noodles and chicken. In small bowl, combine remaining ¼ cup Herb & Garlic Marinade and remaining 1 tablespoon oil. Add just enough dressing to noodle mixture to coat; toss well. Serve with any remaining dressing, if desired. *Makes 4 to 6 servings*

Serving Suggestion: Sprinkle with chopped fresh parsley, if desired.

Hot Off The Grill

Use a meat thermometer to accurately determine the doneness of large cuts of meat or poultry cooked on the rotisserie or covered grill.

Grilled Chicken Pasta Toss

Grilled Rosemary Chicken

2 tablespoons lemon juice
2 tablespoons olive oil
2 cloves garlic, minced
2 tablespoons minced fresh
   rosemary
¼ teaspoon salt
4 boneless skinless chicken
   breasts

1. Whisk together lemon juice, oil, garlic, rosemary and salt in small bowl. Pour into shallow glass dish. Add chicken, turning to coat both sides with lemon juice mixture. Cover and marinate in refrigerator 15 minutes, turning chicken once.

2. Grill chicken over medium-hot coals 5 to 6 minutes per side or until chicken is no longer pink in center.   *Makes 4 servings*

Cook's Notes: For added flavor, moisten a few sprigs of fresh rosemary and toss on the hot coals just before grilling. Store rosemary in the refrigerator for up to five days. Wrap sprigs in a barely damp paper towel and place in a sealed plastic bag.

Prep and Cook Time: *30 minutes*

Sesame-Orange Chicken Skewers

½ cup hoisin sauce
½ cup ketchup
¼ cup seasoned rice vinegar
¼ cup sesame oil
¼ cup orange juice
2 tablespoons drained
   chopped mandarin orange
   segments
1 teaspoon toasted sesame
   seeds
½ teaspoon **LAWRY'S**® Garlic
   Salt
6 boneless, skinless chicken
   breast halves (about
   1½ pounds), cut into
   strips
   Skewers

In large resealable plastic food storage bag, combine all ingredients except chicken; mix well. Remove ¾ cup marinade for basting. Add chicken; seal bag. Marinate in refrigerator at least 1 hour. Remove chicken; discard used marinade. Thread chicken onto skewers. Grill or broil skewers 10 to 15 minutes or until chicken is no longer pink in center and juices run clear when cut, turning once and basting often with additional ¾ cup marinade. *Do not baste during last 5 minutes of cooking.* Discard any remaining marinade.

Makes 6 servings

Serving Suggestion: Serve with steamed rice and snow peas.

Grilled Rosemary Chicken

Chicken Satay with Peanut Sauce

½ cup lime juice
⅓ cup reduced-sodium soy sauce
¼ cup packed brown sugar
4 cloves garlic, minced
¼ teaspoon ground red pepper
3 boneless skinless chicken breast halves (about 1¼ pounds)
18 bamboo skewers (10 to 12 inches long)
¼ cup chunky or creamy peanut butter
¼ cup thick unsweetened coconut milk* or Thick Coconut Milk Substitute (recipe follows)
¼ cup finely chopped onion
1 teaspoon paprika
1 tablespoon finely chopped cilantro

*Coconut milk separates in the can, with thick cream (consistency may be soft like yogurt or firm like shortening) floating to the top over thin, watery milk. Spoon thick cream from top after opening can. If less than ¼ cup, make up difference with remaining coconut milk.

1. Stir lime juice, soy sauce, brown sugar, garlic and red pepper in medium bowl until sugar dissolves. Set ⅓ cup marinade aside in cup.

2. Slice chicken lengthwise into ⅓-inch-thick strips. Add to marinade in bowl and stir to coat evenly.

3. Cover and set aside at room temperature 30 minutes or cover and refrigerate up to 12 hours.

4. Cover skewers with cold water. Soak 20 minutes to prevent them from burning; drain.

5. Place peanut butter in medium bowl. Stir in ⅓ cup reserved marinade, 1 tablespoon at a time, until smooth. Stir in coconut milk, onion and paprika. Transfer sauce to small serving bowl; set aside.

6. Drain chicken; discard marinade. Weave 1 or 2 slices chicken onto each skewer.

7. Grill skewers over hot coals or broil 2 to 3 minutes per side or until chicken is no longer pink in center. Transfer to serving platter.

8. Sprinkle sauce with cilantro; serve with skewers. Garnish as desired.

Makes 6 servings

Thick Coconut Milk Substitute

⅓ cup milk
1 teaspoon cornstarch
½ teaspoon coconut extract

Combine milk and cornstarch in small saucepan. Stir constantly over high heat until mixture boils and thickens. Immediately pour into small bowl; stir in extract.

Chicken Satay with Peanut Sauce

Herbed Butter Chicken

3 tablespoons minced fresh basil
2 teaspoons minced fresh oregano
2 teaspoons minced fresh rosemary
3 tablespoons minced shallots or green onion
2 tablespoons butter, softened
3 cloves garlic, minced
2 teaspoons grated lemon peel
½ teaspoon salt
¼ teaspoon black pepper
4 chicken legs with thighs *or* 1 whole chicken (about 3½ pounds), quartered
1 tablespoon olive oil
Fresh oregano sprigs
Lemon peel strips

Combine herbs, shallots, butter, garlic, lemon peel, salt and pepper in medium bowl. Loosen chicken skin by gently pushing fingers between the skin and chicken, keeping skin intact. Gently rub herb mixture under skin of chicken, forcing it into the leg section; secure skin with wooden picks. (Soak wooden picks in hot water 15 minutes to prevent burning.) Cover and refrigerate chicken at least ½ hour. Brush chicken with oil. Arrange medium KINGSFORD® Briquets on each side of rectangular metal or foil drip pan. Grill chicken, skin side down, in center of grid on covered grill 20 minutes. Turn chicken and cook 20 to 25 minutes or until juices run clear. Garnish with oregano sprigs and lemon strips.

Makes 4 servings

Hot Off The Grill

If you plan on grilling for more than 45 minutes, add 10 to 12 new coals around edges of coals just before you begin to cook. When the new coals are ready, move them to the center of the fire.

Herbed Butter Chicken

Hot and Spicy Thai Ginger Noodles

1¼ cups **LAWRY'S® Thai Ginger Marinade with Lime Juice, divided**
4 **boneless, skinless chicken breast halves (about 1 pound)**
6 **ounces Asian noodles or linguine, cooked**
1 **cup frozen pea pods (about ¼ pound), thawed**
1 **can (5 ounces) sliced water chestnuts, drained**
¼ **cup chopped fresh cilantro**
¼ **cup chopped dry roasted unsalted peanuts**

In large resealable plastic food storage bag, combine 1 cup Thai Ginger Marinade and chicken; seal bag. Marinate in refrigerator at least 30 minutes. Remove chicken; discard used marinade. Grill or broil chicken 10 to 15 minutes or until no longer pink in center and juices run clear when cut, turning halfway through grilling time. Cut chicken into strips. In large bowl, combine chicken, noodles, pea pods, water chestnuts, cilantro and additional ¼ cup Thai Ginger Marinade; toss until well mixed. Sprinkle with peanuts and serve warm.   *Makes 4 to 6 servings*

Serving Suggestion: Serve with peach-flavored iced tea.

Glazed Cornish Hens

¼ **cup A.1.® Bold & Spicy Steak Sauce**
¼ **cup currant jelly**
2 **tablespoons red cooking wine**
2 **cloves garlic, crushed**
2 **teaspoons cornstarch**
2 **(1½-pound) Cornish game hens, halved lengthwise with back bones removed**

In small saucepan, over medium heat, cook and stir steak sauce, jelly, wine, garlic and cornstarch until thickened; cool.

Grill or broil hens, beginning with skin side up, over medium heat 35 to 45 minutes or until done, turning and brushing occasionally with prepared glaze. Serve hot.   *Makes 4 servings*

Hot and Spicy Thai Ginger Noodles

Jamaican Grilled Chicken

**1 whole chicken (4 pounds),
   cut into pieces or 6 whole
   chicken legs**
**1 cup coarsely chopped fresh
   cilantro leaves and stems**
**½ cup FRANK'S® Original
   REDHOT® Cayenne
   Pepper Sauce**
⅓ cup vegetable oil
**6 cloves garlic, coarsely
   chopped**
**¼ cup fresh lime juice (juice of
   2 limes)**
1 teaspoon grated lime peel
1 teaspoon ground turmeric
1 teaspoon ground allspice

1. Loosen and pull back skin from chicken pieces. Do not remove skin. Place chicken pieces in large resealable plastic food storage bags or large glass bowl.

2. Place remaining ingredients in blender or food processor. Process until smooth. Reserve ⅓ cup marinade. Pour remaining marinade over chicken pieces, turning to coat evenly. Seal bags or cover bowl; refrigerate 1 hour.

3. Prepare grill. Reposition skin on chicken pieces. Place chicken on oiled grid. Grill, over medium to medium-low coals, 45 minutes or until chicken is no longer pink near bone and juices run clear, turning and basting often with reserved marinade.

Makes 6 servings

Prep Time: *15 minutes*
Marinate Time: *1 hour*
Cook Time: *45 minutes*

Caribbean Jerk Chicken with Quick Fruit Salsa

**1 cup plus 2 tablespoons
   LAWRY'S® Caribbean Jerk
   Marinade with Papaya
   Juice, divided**
**1 can (15¼ ounces) tropical
   fruit salad, drained**
**4 boneless, skinless chicken
   breast halves (about
   1 pound)**

In small glass bowl, combine 2 tablespoons Caribbean Jerk Marinade and tropical fruit; mix well and set aside. In large resealable plastic food storage bag, combine additional 1 cup Caribbean Jerk Marinade and chicken; seal bag. Marinate in refrigerator at least 30 minutes. Remove chicken; discard used marinade. Grill or broil chicken 10 to 15 minutes or until no longer pink in center and juices run clear when cut, turning halfway through grilling time. Top chicken with fruit salsa.

Makes 4 servings

Serving Suggestion: Serve with hot cooked rice and black beans.

Jamaican Grilled Chicken

Japanese Yakitori

**1 pound boneless skinless
    chicken breast halves, cut
    into ¾-inch-wide strips**
**2 tablespoons sherry or
    canned pineapple juice**
**2 tablespoons reduced-
    sodium soy sauce**
1 tablespoon sugar
1 tablespoon peanut oil
½ teaspoon minced garlic
½ teaspoon minced ginger
5 ounces red pearl onions
**½ fresh pineapple, cut into
    1-inch wedges**

1. Place chicken in large heavy-duty resealable plastic food storage bag. Combine sherry, soy sauce, sugar, oil, garlic and ginger in small bowl; mix thoroughly to dissolve sugar. Pour into plastic bag with chicken; seal bag and turn to coat thoroughly. Refrigerate 30 minutes or up to 2 hours, turning occasionally. (If using wooden or bamboo skewers, prepare by soaking skewers in water 20 to 30 minutes to keep from burning.)

2. Meanwhile, place onions in boiling water 4 minutes; drain and cool in ice water to stop cooking. Cut off root ends and slip off outer skins; set aside.

3. Drain chicken, reserving marinade. Weave chicken accordion-style onto skewers, alternating onions and pineapple with chicken. Brush with reserved marinade; discard remaining marinade.

4. Grill on uncovered grill over medium-hot coals 6 to 8 minutes or until chicken is no longer pink in center, turning once.

Makes 6 servings

Persian Chicken Breasts

1 medium lemon
2 teaspoons olive oil
1 teaspoon ground cinnamon
½ teaspoon salt
**¼ teaspoon ground black
    pepper**
¼ teaspoon turmeric
**4 boneless skinless chicken
    breast halves**
4 flour tortillas or soft lavash

1. Peel lemon rind into long strips with paring knife; reserve for garnish, if desired. Juice lemon and combine juice with oil, cinnamon, salt, pepper and turmeric in large heavy-duty resealable plastic food storage bag. Gently massage ingredients in bag to mix thoroughly; add chicken. Seal bag and turn to coat thoroughly. Refrigerate 4 hours or overnight.

2. Remove chicken from marinade and gently shake to remove excess. Grill chicken 5 to 7 minutes per side or until chicken is no longer pink in center, brushing occasionally with marinade. Discard remaining marinade. Serve chicken with lightly grilled tortillas or lavash and red and yellow grilled peppers. Garnish as desired.

Makes 4 servings

Japanese Yakitori

Mediterranean Chicken Kabobs

2 pounds boneless skinless chicken breasts or chicken tenders, cut into 1-inch pieces

1 small eggplant, peeled and cut into 1-inch pieces

1 medium zucchini, cut crosswise into ½-inch slices

2 medium onions, each cut into 8 wedges

16 medium mushrooms, stems removed

16 cherry tomatoes

1 cup defatted low-sodium chicken broth

⅔ cup balsamic vinegar

3 tablespoons olive oil or vegetable oil

2 tablespoons dried mint leaves

4 teaspoons dried basil leaves

1 tablespoon dried oregano leaves

2 teaspoons grated lemon peel

Chopped fresh parsley (optional)

4 cups hot cooked couscous

1. Alternately thread chicken, eggplant, zucchini, onions, mushrooms and tomatoes onto 16 metal skewers; place in large glass baking dish.

2. Combine chicken broth, vinegar, oil, mint, basil and oregano in small bowl; pour over kabobs. Cover; marinate in refrigerator 2 hours, turning kabobs occasionally.

3. Broil kabobs, 6 inches from heat source, 10 to 15 minutes or until chicken is no longer pink in center, turning kabobs halfway through cooking time. Or, grill kabobs, on covered grill over medium-hot coals, 10 to 15 minutes or until chicken is no longer pink in center, turning kabobs halfway through cooking time. Stir lemon peel and parsley into couscous; serve with kabobs.

Makes 8 servings
(2 kabobs per serving)

Hot Off The Grill

Store charcoal in a dry place. Charcoal won't burn well if it is damp.

Mediterranean Chicken Kabobs

Mesquite Grilled Chicken in Cornbread Bundles

¾ cup **LAWRY'S**® Mesquite
    Marinade with Lime Juice
4 boneless, skinless chicken
    breast halves (about
    1 pound)
½ cup chopped red bell pepper
½ cup toasted pine nuts, finely
    chopped
¼ cup toasted walnuts, finely
    chopped (optional)
1 can (7 ounces) diced mild
    green chiles, drained
1 tablespoon lime juice
½ teaspoon **LAWRY'S**®
    Seasoned Salt
½ teaspoon **LAWRY'S**® Garlic
    Powder with Parsley
2 packages (11 ounces each)
    refrigerated cornstick or
    breadstick dough
1 egg white, beaten

In large resealable plastic food storage bag, combine Mesquite Marinade and chicken; seal bag. Marinate in refrigerator at least 30 minutes. Remove chicken; discard used marinade. Grill or broil chicken 10 to 15 minutes or until no longer pink in center and juices run clear when cut, turning halfway through grilling time. In small bowl, combine bell pepper, nuts, chiles, lime juice, Seasoned Salt and Garlic Powder with Parsley; mix well. Roll out dough into 4 equal squares. On each square, place 1 chicken breast and ¼ of nut mixture. Fold dough to enclose; pinch edges to seal. Brush tops with egg white. Bake in 350°F. oven about 10 to 15 minutes or until golden and puffy.   *Makes 4 servings*

Serving Suggestion: Serve with cucumber slices and french-fried potatoes.

Hot Off The Grill

NEVER use alcohol, gasoline or kerosene to start a fire—all three can cause an explosion.

Mesquite Grilled Chicken in Cornbread Bundles

Orange-Mint Chicken

2 teaspoons LAWRY'S®
    Seasoned Salt
1 broiler-fryer chicken
    (2½ to 3 pounds), cut into
    halves
½ cup orange marmalade
3 tablespoons butter
3 tablespoons honey
1 teaspoon dried mint,
    crushed

Sprinkle Seasoned Salt over chicken. Let stand 10 to 15 minutes. In medium saucepan, combine marmalade, butter, honey and mint. Heat 1 to 2 minutes, stirring frequently. Grill or broil chicken 35 to 45 minutes or until no longer pink in center and juices run clear when cut, turning once and basting often with marmalade mixture. *Do not baste during last 5 minutes of cooking.* Discard any remaining marmalade mixture. *Makes 4 to 6 servings*

Serving Suggestion: Serve with wild rice pilaf and garnish with orange wedges and fresh mint, if desired.

Barbecued Chicken with Chili-Orange Glaze

1 to 2 dried de arbol chilies*
1½ teaspoons shredded orange
    peel
½ cup fresh orange juice
2 tablespoons tequila
2 cloves garlic, minced
¼ teaspoon salt
¼ cup vegetable oil
1 broiler-fryer chicken (about
    3 pounds), cut into
    quarters
    Orange slices (optional)
    Cilantro sprigs (optional)

For milder flavor, discard seeds from chili peppers. Since chili peppers can sting and irritate the skin, wear rubber gloves when handling peppers and do not touch eyes.

Crush chilies into coarse flakes in mortar with pestle. Combine chilies, orange peel, orange juice, tequila, garlic and salt in small bowl. Gradually add oil, whisking continuously, until marinade is thoroughly blended.

Arrange chicken in single layer in shallow glass baking dish. Pour marinade over chicken; turn pieces to coat. Marinate, covered, in refrigerator 2 to 3 hours, turning chicken over and basting with marinade several times.

Prepare charcoal grill for direct cooking or preheat broiler. Drain chicken, reserving marinade. Bring marinade to a boil in small saucepan over high heat. Grill chicken on covered grill or broil, 6 to 8 inches from heat, 15 minutes, brushing frequently with marinade. Turn chicken over. Grill or broil 15 minutes more or until chicken is no longer pink in center and juices run clear, brushing frequently with marinade. *Do not baste for last 5 minutes of grilling.* Garnish with orange slices and cilantro, if desired.

Makes 4 servings

Orange-Mint Chicken

Pesto-Stuffed Grilled Chicken

2 tablespoons pine nuts or walnuts
2 cloves garlic, peeled
½ cup packed fresh basil leaves
¼ teaspoon black pepper
5 tablespoons extra-virgin olive oil, divided
¼ cup grated Parmesan cheese
1 fresh or thawed frozen roasting chicken or capon (6 to 7 pounds)
2 tablespoons fresh lemon juice
Additional fresh basil leaves and fresh red currants for garnish

Preheat oven to 350°F. To toast pine nuts, spread in single layer on baking sheet. Bake 8 to 10 minutes or until golden brown, stirring frequently. Remove pine nuts from baking sheet; cool completely. Set aside.

Prepare grill with rectangular metal or foil drip pan. Bank briquets on either side of drip pan for indirect cooking.

Meanwhile, to prepare pesto, drop garlic through feed tube of food processor with motor running. Add basil, pine nuts and black pepper; process until basil is minced. With processor running, add 3 tablespoons oil in slow, steady stream until smooth paste forms, scraping down side of bowl once. Add cheese; process until well blended.

Remove giblets from chicken cavity; reserve for another use. Rinse chicken with cold water; pat dry with paper towels. Loosen skin over breast of chicken by pushing fingers between skin and meat, taking care not to tear skin. Do not loosen skin over wings and drumsticks. Using rubber spatula or small spoon, spread pesto under breast skin; massage skin to evenly spread pesto. Combine remaining 2 tablespoons oil and lemon juice in small bowl; brush over chicken skin. Insert meat thermometer into center of thickest part of thigh, not touching bone. Tuck wings under back; tie legs together with wet kitchen string. Place chicken, breast side up, on grid directly over drip pan. Grill, on covered grill, over medium-low coals 1 hour 10 minutes to 1 hour 30 minutes or until thermometer registers 185°F, adding 4 to 9 briquets to both sides of the fire after 45 minutes to maintain medium-low coals. Transfer chicken to carving board; tent with foil. Let stand 15 minutes before carving. Garnish, if desired. *Makes 6 servings*

Pesto-Stuffed Grilled Chicken

Rotelle with Grilled Chicken Dijon

¾ cup **GREY POUPON®** Dijon
    Mustard, divided
1 **tablespoon lemon juice**
1 **tablespoon olive oil**
1 **clove garlic, minced**
½ **teaspoon Italian seasoning**
1 **pound boneless, skinless**
    chicken breasts
¼ cup **PARKAY®** 70% **Vegetable**
    Oil Spread
1 cup **COLLEGE INN®**
    Chicken Broth or Lower
    Sodium Chicken Broth
1 **cup chopped cooked**
    broccoli
⅓ **cup coarsely chopped**
    roasted red peppers
1 **pound tri-color rotelle or**
    spiral-shaped pasta,
    cooked
¼ **cup grated Parmesan**
    cheese

In medium bowl, combine ¼ cup mustard, lemon juice, oil, garlic and Italian seasoning. Add chicken, stirring to coat well. Refrigerate for 1 hour.

Grill or broil chicken over medium heat for 6 minutes on each side or until done. Cool slightly; slice into ½-inch strips and set aside.

In large skillet, over medium heat, melt spread; blend in remaining mustard and chicken broth. Stir in broccoli and peppers; heat through. In large serving bowl, combine hot cooked pasta, broccoli mixture, chicken and Parmesan cheese, tossing to coat well. Garnish as desired. Serve immediately.   *Makes 5 servings*

Hot Off The Grill

The coals are ready when they are about 80% ash gray during daylight and glowing at night.

Rotelle with Grilled Chicken Dijon

Southwest Chicken

2 tablespoons olive oil
I clove garlic, pressed
I teaspoon chili powder
I teaspoon ground cumin
I teaspoon dried oregano
  leaves
½ teaspoon salt
I pound skinless boneless
  chicken breast halves or
  thighs

Combine oil, garlic, chili powder, cumin, oregano and salt; brush over both sides of chicken to coat. Grill chicken over medium-hot KINGSFORD® Briquets 8 to 10 minutes or until chicken is no longer pink, turning once. Serve immediately or use in Build a Burrito, Taco Salad or other favorite recipes.   *Makes 4 servings*

Build a Burrito: Top warm large flour tortillas with strips of Southwest Chicken and your choice of drained canned black beans, cooked brown or white rice, shredded cheese, salsa verde, shredded lettuce, sliced black olives and chopped cilantro. Fold in sides and roll to enclose filling. Heat in microwave oven at HIGH until heated through. (Or, wrap in foil and heat in preheated 350°F oven.)

Taco Salad: For a quick one-dish meal, layer strips of Southwest Chicken with tomato wedges, blue or traditional corn tortilla chips, sliced black olives, shredded romaine or iceberg lettuce, shredded cheese and avocado slices. Serve with salsa, sour cream, guacamole or a favorite dressing.

Hot Off The Grill

Southwest Chicken can be grilled ahead and refrigerated for several days or frozen for longer storage.

Southwest Chicken

Spicy Mango Chicken

¼ cup mango nectar
¼ cup chopped fresh cilantro
2 jalapeño chile peppers,*
    seeded and finely chopped
2 teaspoons vegetable oil
2 teaspoons **LAWRY'S®**
    Seasoned Salt
½ teaspoon **LAWRY'S® Garlic**
    Powder with Parsley
½ teaspoon ground cumin
4 boneless, skinless chicken
    breast halves (about
    1 pound)
Mango & Black Bean Salsa
    (recipe follows)

Jalapeño peppers can sting and irritate the skin; wear rubber gloves when handling peppers and do not touch eyes.

In small bowl, combine all ingredients except chicken and salsa; mix well. Brush marinade on both sides of chicken. Grill or broil chicken 10 to 15 minutes or until no longer pink in center and juices run clear when cut, turning once and basting often with additional marinade. *Do not baste during last 5 minutes of cooking.* Discard any remaining marinade. Top chicken with Mango & Black Bean Salsa. *Makes 4 servings*

Mango & Black Bean Salsa

1 ripe mango, peeled, seeded and chopped
1 cup canned black beans, rinsed and drained
½ cup chopped tomato
2 thinly sliced green onions
1 tablespoon chopped fresh cilantro
1½ teaspoons lime juice
1½ teaspoons red wine vinegar
½ teaspoon **LAWRY'S®** Seasoned Salt

In medium bowl, combine all ingredients; mix well. Let stand 30 minutes to allow flavors to blend. *Makes about 2¾ cups*

Serving Suggestion: Serve with green beans.

Spicy Mango Chicken

Rotisserie Chicken with Pesto Brush

2 BUTTERBALL® Fresh Young Roasters
¼ **cup chopped fresh oregano**
¼ **cup chopped fresh parsley**
2 **tablespoons chopped fresh rosemary**
2 **tablespoons chopped fresh thyme**
½ **cup olive oil**
½ **cup balsamic vinegar**

Combine oregano, parsley, rosemary, thyme, oil and vinegar in small bowl. Roast chicken according to rotisserie directions. Dip brush into herb mixture; brush chicken with herb mixture every 30 minutes for first 2 hours of roasting. Brush every 15 minutes during last hour of roasting. Roast chicken until internal temperature reaches 180°F in thigh and meat is no longer pink.

Serves 16

Tip: To make an aromatic herb brush, bundle sprigs of rosemary, thyme, oregano and parsley together. Tie bundle with kitchen string. Use as brush for pesto.

Preparation Time: *15 minutes plus roasting time*

Lemon Pepper Chicken

¼ **cup olive oil**
¼ **cup finely chopped onion**
2 **teaspoons grated lemon peel**
⅓ **cup lemon juice**
1 **tablespoon cracked black pepper**
1 **tablespoon brown sugar**
¾ **teaspoon salt**
3 **cloves garlic, minced**
4 **chicken quarters (about 2½ pounds)**

Combine oil, onion, lemon peel, lemon juice, pepper, sugar, salt and garlic in small bowl; reserve 2 tablespoons marinade. Combine remaining marinade and chicken in large resealable plastic food storage bag. Seal bag; knead to coat. Refrigerate at least 4 hours or overnight.

Remove chicken from marinade; discard marinade. Arrange chicken on microwavable plate; cover with waxed paper. Microwave at HIGH 5 minutes. Turn and rearrange chicken. Cover and microwave at HIGH 5 minutes more.

Transfer chicken to grill. Grill covered over medium-hot coals 15 to 20 minutes or until juices run clear, turning several times and basting often with reserved marinade. *Makes 4 servings*

Rotisserie Chicken with Pesto Brush

Summer Raspberry Chicken

4 boneless, skinless chicken breast halves (about 1 pound), pounded to ¼-inch thickness
¾ cup LAWRY'S® Dijon & Honey Marinade with Lemon Juice, divided
1 cup fresh or frozen raspberries
½ cup walnut pieces

Grill or broil chicken 10 to 15 minutes or until no longer pink in center and juices run clear when cut, turning once and basting often with ½ cup Dijon & Honey Marinade. *Do not baste during last 5 minutes of cooking.* Discard any remaining marinade. Cut chicken into strips. In food processor or blender, process raspberries and additional ¼ cup Dijon & Honey Marinade 10 seconds. Drizzle raspberry sauce over chicken; sprinkle with walnuts.

Makes 4 servings

Serving Suggestion: Serve chicken on field greens or angel hair pasta. Garnish with fresh raspberries, if desired.

Grilled Marinated Chicken

8 whole chicken legs (thighs and drumsticks attached) (about 3½ pounds)
6 ounces frozen lemonade concentrate, thawed
2 tablespoons white wine vinegar
1 tablespoon grated lemon peel
2 cloves garlic, minced

1. Remove skin and all visible fat from chicken. Place chicken in 13×9-inch glass baking dish. Combine remaining ingredients in small bowl; blend well. Pour over chicken; turn to coat. Cover; refrigerate 3 hours or overnight, turning occasionally.

2. To prevent sticking, spray grid with nonstick cooking spray. Prepare coals for grilling.

3. Place chicken on grill 4 inches from medium-hot coals. Grill 20 to 30 minutes or until chicken is no longer pink near bone, turning occasionally. (Do not overcook or chicken will be dry.) Garnish with curly endive and lemon peel strips, if desired.

Makes 8 servings

Summer Raspberry Chicken

Thai Barbecued Chicken

2 jalapeño peppers*
1 cup coarsely chopped cilantro
2 tablespoons fish sauce
8 cloves garlic, peeled and coarsely chopped
1 tablespoon packed brown sugar
1 teaspoon curry powder
Grated peel of 1 lemon
1 cut-up frying chicken (about 3 pounds)

Jalapeños can sting and irritate the skin; wear rubber gloves when handling peppers and do not touch eyes. Wash hands after handling.

Cut jalapeños lengthwise into halves. Scrape out and discard stems, seeds and veins. Cut peppers into coarse pieces. Place jalapeños, cilantro, fish sauce, garlic, brown sugar, curry powder and lemon peel in blender or food processor; blend to form coarse paste.

Rinse chicken pieces; pat dry with paper towels. Work fingers between skin and meat on breast and thigh pieces. Rub about 1 teaspoon seasoning paste under skin on each piece. Rub chicken pieces on all sides with remaining paste. Place chicken in large resealable plastic food storage bag or covered container; marinate in refrigerator 3 to 4 hours or overnight.

Prepare coals for grill.** Brush grid lightly with oil. Grill chicken over medium coals, skin side down, about 10 minutes or until well browned. Turn chicken and grill 20 to 30 minutes more or until breast meat is no longer pink in center and thigh meat at bone is no longer pink. (Thighs and legs may require 10 to 15 minutes more cooking time than breasts.) If chicken is browned on both sides but still needs additional cooking, move to edge of grill, away from direct heat, to finish cooking. Garnish as desired.

Makes 4 servings

**To cook in oven, place chicken skin side up in lightly oiled baking pan. Bake in preheated 375°F oven 30 to 45 minutes or until no longer pink in center.*

Thai Barbecued Chicken

Thai Grilled Chicken

4 boneless chicken breast
    halves, skinned if desired
    (about 1¼ pounds)
¼ cup soy sauce
2 teaspoons bottled minced
    garlic
½ teaspoon red pepper flakes
2 tablespoons honey
1 tablespoon fresh lime juice

1. Prepare grill for grilling. Place chicken in shallow dish or plate. Combine soy sauce, garlic and pepper flakes in measuring cup. Pour over chicken, turning to coat. Let stand 10 minutes.

2. Meanwhile, combine honey and lime juice in small bowl until blended; set aside.

3. Place chicken on grid over medium coals; brush with some of marinade remaining in dish. Discard remaining marinade. Grill over covered grill 5 minutes. Brush chicken with half of honey mixture; turn and brush with remaining honey mixture. Grill 5 minutes more or until chicken is cooked through. *Makes 4 servings*

Serving Suggestion: Serve with steamed white rice, Oriental vegetables and fresh fruit salad.

Prep/Cook Time: *25 minutes*

Chicken and Fruit Kabobs

1¾ cups honey
¾ cup fresh lemon juice
½ cup Dijon-style mustard
⅓ cup chopped fresh ginger
4 pounds boneless skinless
    chicken breasts, cut up
6 fresh plums, pitted and
    quartered
3 firm bananas, cut into
    chunks
4 cups fresh pineapple chunks
    (about half of medium
    pineapple)

Combine honey, lemon juice, mustard and ginger in small bowl; mix well. Thread chicken and fruit onto skewers, alternating chicken with fruit; brush generously with honey mixture. Place kabobs on grill about 4 inches from heat. Grill 10 minutes or until chicken is no longer pink in center, turning and brushing frequently with remaining honey mixture. *Makes 12 servings*

Thai Grilled Chicken

Jamaican Rum Chicken

½ **cup dark rum**
2 tablespoons lime juice or
lemon juice
2 tablespoons soy sauce
2 tablespoons brown sugar
4 large cloves garlic, minced
1 to 2 jalapeño chilies, seeded
and minced
1 tablespoon minced fresh
ginger
1 teaspoon dried thyme
leaves, crushed
½ **teaspoon black pepper**
6 boneless skinless chicken
breast halves

1. To prepare marinade, combine rum, lime juice, soy sauce, sugar, garlic, chilies, ginger, thyme and black pepper in 2-quart glass measuring cup.

2. Rinse chicken and pat dry with paper towels. Place chicken in resealable plastic food storage bag. Pour marinade over chicken. Press air out of bag and seal tightly. Turn bag over to completely coat chicken with marinade. Refrigerate 4 hours or overnight, turning bag once or twice.

3. Prepare barbecue grill for direct grilling by spreading hot coals in single layer that extends 1 to 2 inches beyond area of food.

4. Drain chicken; reserve marinade. Place chicken on grid. Grill chicken, on uncovered grill, over medium-hot coals 6 minutes per side or until chicken is no longer pink in center.

5. Meanwhile, bring remaining marinade to a boil in small saucepan over medium-high heat. Boil 5 minutes or until marinade is reduced by about half.

6. To serve, drizzle marinade over chicken. Garnish as desired.

Makes 6 servings

Jamaican Rum Chicken

Turkey Cutlets with Chipotle Pepper Mole

1 package **BUTTERBALL®**
    Fresh Boneless Turkey
    Breast Cutlets
1 can (14½ ounces) chicken
    broth
¼ cup raisins
4 cloves garlic, minced
1 chipotle chile pepper in
    adobo sauce
2 tablespoons ground
    almonds
2 teaspoons unsweetened
    cocoa
½ cup chopped fresh cilantro
2 tablespoons fresh lime juice
½ teaspoon salt

To prepare chipotle sauce, combine chicken broth, raisins, garlic, chile pepper, almonds and cocoa in medium saucepan. Simmer over low heat 10 minutes. Pour into food processor or blender; process until smooth. Add cilantro, lime juice and salt. Grill cutlets according to package directions. Serve chipotle sauce over grilled cutlets with Mexican polenta.*   Serves 7

*To make Mexican polenta, cook 1 cup instant cornmeal polenta according to package directions. Stir in ½ teaspoon garlic powder, ½ teaspoon salt and 2 cups taco-seasoned cheese.

Preparation Time: 20 minutes

Hot Off The Grill

Remember, hot coals create a hot grill, grid, tools and food. Always wear heavy-duty fireproof mitts to protect your hands.

Turkey Cutlets with Chipotle Pepper Mole

Turkey Teriyaki with Grilled Mushrooms

1¼ pounds turkey breast slices, tenderloins or medallions
¼ cup sake or sherry wine
¼ cup soy sauce
3 tablespoons granulated sugar, brown sugar or honey
1 piece (1-inch cube) fresh ginger, minced
3 cloves garlic, minced
1 tablespoon vegetable oil
½ pound mushrooms
4 green onions, cut into 2-inch pieces

Cut turkey into long 2-inch-wide strips.* Combine sake, soy sauce, sugar, ginger, garlic and oil in 2-quart glass dish. Add turkey; turn to coat. Cover and refrigerate 15 minutes or overnight. Remove turkey from marinade; discard marinade. Thread turkey onto metal or wooden skewers, alternating with mushrooms and green onions. (Soak wooden skewers in hot water 30 minutes to prevent burning.) Grill on covered grill over medium-hot KINGSFORD® Briquets about 3 minutes per side until turkey is cooked through.

Makes 4 servings

*Do not cut tenderloins or medallions.

Grilled Herbed Turkey Tenderloins

½ cup A.1.® Steak Sauce
2 tablespoons dry sherry
2 tablespoons honey
2 tablespoons olive oil
1 tablespoon lemon juice
1 teaspoon rosemary leaves, crushed
½ teaspoon ground sage
2 pounds turkey tenderloins

In small bowl, combine steak sauce, sherry, honey, oil, lemon juice, rosemary and sage; reserve ½ cup sauce mixture. Place turkey tenderloins in glass dish; coat with remaining sauce. Cover; chill 1 hour, turning occasionally.

Remove turkey from marinade. Grill turkey over medium heat 25 to 35 minutes or until done, turning occasionally. Meanwhile, in small saucepan, over medium heat, heat reserved sauce. Slice turkey; serve with warm sauce.

Makes 6 to 8 servings

Turkey Teriyaki with Grilled Mushrooms

Mesquite-Grilled Turkey

2 cups mesquite chips,
   divided
1 fresh or thawed frozen
   turkey (10 to 12 pounds)
1 small sweet or Spanish
   onion, peeled and
   quartered
1 lemon, quartered
3 fresh tarragon sprigs
1 metal skewer (6 inches long)
2 tablespoons butter or
   margarine, softened
   Salt and pepper (optional)
   Additional fresh tarragon
   sprigs (optional)
¼ cup butter or margarine,
   melted
2 tablespoons fresh lemon
   juice
2 tablespoons chopped fresh
   tarragon leaves *or* 2
   teaspoons dried tarragon
   leaves, crushed
2 cloves garlic, minced

1. Prepare barbecue grill with rectangular metal or foil drip pan. Bank briquets on either side of drip pan for indirect cooking.

2. Meanwhile, cover mesquite chips with cold water; soak 20 minutes.

3. Remove giblets from turkey cavity; reserve for another use. Rinse turkey with cold running water; pat dry with paper towels. Place onion, lemon and 3 tarragon sprigs in cavity. Pull skin over neck; secure with metal skewer. Tuck wing tips under back; tie legs together with wet kitchen string.

4. Using fingers or paper towel, spread softened butter over turkey skin; sprinkle with salt and pepper to taste. Insert meat thermometer into center of thickest part of thigh, not touching bone.

5. Drain mesquite chips; sprinkle 1 cup over coals. Place turkey, breast side up, on grid directly over drip pan. Grill turkey, on covered grill, over medium coals 11 to 14 minutes per pound, adding 4 to 9 briquets to both sides of fire each hour to maintain medium coals and adding remaining 1 cup mesquite chips after 1 hour of grilling.

6. Meanwhile, soak additional fresh tarragon sprigs in water.

7. Combine melted butter, lemon juice, chopped tarragon and garlic in small bowl. Brush half of mixture over turkey during last 30 minutes of grilling. Place soaked tarragon sprigs directly on coals. Continue to grill, covered, 20 minutes. Brush with remaining mixture. Continue to grill, covered, about 10 minutes or until thermometer registers 185°F.

8. Transfer turkey to carving board; tent with foil. Let stand 15 minutes before carving. Discard onion, lemon and tarragon sprigs from cavity.

Makes 8 to 10 servings

Mesquite-Grilled Turkey

Hidden Herb Grilled Turkey Breast

1 (3- to 9-pound)
BUTTERBALL® Breast of
Young Turkey, thawed
¼ cup chopped fresh parsley
2 tablespoons chopped mixed
fresh herbs such as thyme,
oregano and marjoram
2 tablespoons grated
Parmesan cheese
1 teaspoon olive oil
½ teaspoon lemon juice
½ teaspoon salt
¼ teaspoon garlic powder
¼ teaspoon black pepper
Vegetable oil

Prepare grill for indirect-heat grilling. Combine parsley, herbs, Parmesan cheese, oil, lemon juice, salt, garlic powder and pepper in medium bowl. Gently loosen and lift turkey skin from surface of meat. Spread herb blend evenly over breast meat. Replace skin over herb blend. Brush skin with vegetable oil. Place turkey breast skin side up on prepared grill. Cover grill and cook 1½ to 2½ hours for a 3- to 9-pound breast or until internal temperature reaches 170°F and meat is no longer pink in center.

Number of servings varies

Preparation Time: *15 minutes plus grilling time*

Caribbean Grilled Turkey

1 package BUTTERBALL®
Fresh Boneless Turkey
Breast Tenderloins
4 green onions
4 cloves garlic
2 tablespoons peach preserves
2 tablespoons fresh lime juice
1 teaspoon *each* salt, bottled
hot sauce, soy sauce
1 teaspoon shredded lime
peel
¼ teaspoon black pepper

Lightly spray unheated grill rack with nonstick cooking spray. Prepare grill for medium-direct-heat cooking. In food processor or blender, process onions, garlic, preserves, lime juice, salt, hot sauce, soy sauce, lime peel and pepper until smooth. Spread over tenderloins. Place tenderloins on rack over medium-hot grill. Grill 20 minutes or until meat is no longer pink, turning frequently for even browning.

Makes 6 servings

Preparation Time: *25 minutes*

Hidden Herb Grilled Turkey Breast

Grilled Turkey with Walnut Pesto Sauce

**1 (4- to 5½-pound) turkey
   breast
   Walnut Pesto Sauce (recipe
   follows)**

• Prepare coals for grilling.

• Place aluminum drip pan in center of charcoal grate under grilling rack. Arrange hot coals around drip pan.

• Place turkey on greased grill. Grill, covered, 1½ to 2 hours or until internal temperature reaches 170°F.

• Slice turkey; serve with Walnut Pesto Sauce. Garnish with red and yellow pear-shaped cherry tomatoes, fresh chives and basil leaves, if desired.   *Makes 12 servings*

Prep Time: *15 minutes*
Cook Time: *2 hours*

Walnut Pesto Sauce

**1 (8-ounce) container LIGHT® Light Soft
   PHILADELPHIA Cream Cheese
1 (7-ounce) container refrigerated prepared pesto
½ cup finely chopped walnuts, toasted
⅓ cup milk
1 garlic clove, minced
⅛ teaspoon ground red pepper**

• Stir together all ingredients in small bowl until well blended. Serve chilled or at room temperature.

Grilled Turkey with Walnut Pesto Sauce

Mesquite Turkey Kabobs with Fresh Rosemary

1½ cups **LAWRY'S®** Mesquite Marinade with Lime Juice, divided
1¼ pounds turkey cutlets, cut into 2½×1-inch strips
½ ounce fresh rosemary, cut into 1-inch sprigs
1 yellow bell pepper, cut into chunks
1 red bell pepper, cut into chunks
1 red onion, cut into thin wedges
Skewers

In large resealable plastic food storage bag, combine 1 cup Mesquite Marinade and turkey; seal bag. Marinate in refrigerator at least 30 minutes. Remove turkey; discard used marinade. Place rosemary sprig in center of each turkey piece; fold turkey in half enclosing rosemary sprig. Alternately thread turkey, bell peppers and onion onto skewers. Grill or broil skewers 10 to 15 minutes or until turkey is no longer pink in center and juices run clear when cut, turning once and basting often with additional ½ cup Mesquite Marinade. *Do not baste during last 5 minutes of cooking.* Discard any remaining marinade. *Makes 4 servings*

Serving Suggestion: Serve over bed of herbed brown rice with a tossed green salad.

Hot Off The Grill

The number of coals required for barbecuing depends on the size and type of grill and amount of food to be prepared. As a general rule, it takes about 30 coals to grill one pound of meat.

Mesquite Turkey Kabobs with Fresh Rosemary

Maple-Glazed Turkey Breast

1 bone-in turkey breast
    (5 to 6 pounds)
Roast rack (optional)
¼ cup pure maple syrup
2 tablespoons butter or
    margarine, melted
1 tablespoon bourbon
    (optional)
2 teaspoons freshly grated
    orange peel
Fresh bay leaves for garnish

1. Prepare barbecue grill with rectangular metal or foil drip pan. Bank briquets on either side of drip pan for indirect cooking.

2. Insert meat thermometer into center of thickest part of turkey breast, not touching bone. Place turkey, bone side down, on roast rack or directly on grid, directly over drip pan. Grill turkey, on covered grill, over medium coals 55 minutes, adding 4 to 9 briquets to both sides of fire after 45 minutes to maintain medium coals.

3. Combine maple syrup, butter, bourbon and orange peel in small bowl; brush half of mixture over turkey. Continue to grill, covered, 10 minutes. Brush with remaining mixture; continue to grill, covered, about 10 minutes or until thermometer registers 170°F.

4. Transfer turkey to carving board; tent with foil. Let stand 10 minutes before carving. Cut turkey into thin slices. Garnish, if desired.   *Makes 6 to 8 servings*

Variation: For hickory-smoked flavor, cover 2 cups hickory chips with cold water; soak 20 minutes. Drain; sprinkle over coals just before placing turkey on grid.

Maple-Glazed Turkey Breast

Smoked Barbecued Turkey

1 turkey (10 to 12 pounds)
1 quart water
1 quart orange juice
1 cup honey
½ cup **LAWRY'S®** Seasoned
    Salt
2 oranges, cut into quarters
2 limes, cut into quarters
2 tablespoons pickling spices
    Barbecue Sauce (recipe
    follows)

In large glass bowl, place turkey. In large saucepan, combine next 7 ingredients; bring to a boil, stirring occasionally. Remove from heat; cool. Pour over turkey; cover. Marinate in refrigerator 4 to 6 hours. Remove turkey; discard used marinade. Secure wings behind back and tie legs and tail together with cotton string. Place turkey, breast side up, in center of smoker grill directly over drip pan. Grill, using indirect heat method, 13 to 15 minutes per pound (about 2 to 3 hours) or until internal temperature reaches 185°F. and juices run clear when cut. Remove from grill and place on rack in large pan; brush with warm Barbecue Sauce. Bake in 375°F. oven 10 minutes.

Makes 10 servings

Barbecue Sauce

  2 tablespoons vegetable oil
½ cup finely chopped onion
  1 teaspoon **LAWRY'S®** Garlic Powder with Parsley
½ cup ketchup
½ cup white wine vinegar
½ cup lemon juice
½ cup honey
¼ cup white Worcestershire sauce
  2 teaspoons dry mustard
1½ teaspoons **LAWRY'S®** Seasoned Salt
½ teaspoon ground red pepper

In small saucepan, heat oil; add onion and Garlic Powder with Parsley and cook until tender. Add remaining ingredients; bring to a boil. Reduce heat to low; cook 10 to 15 minutes.

Makes 2½ cups

Serving Suggestion: Ladle Barbecue Sauce over sliced turkey.

Smoked Barbecued Turkey

Sure-Fire Seafood

Lobster Tail with Tasty Butter (page 312)

Beach Grill (page 316)

Barbecued Salmon

4 salmon steaks, ¾ to 1 inch thick
3 tablespoons lemon juice
2 tablespoons soy sauce
  Salt and black pepper
½ cup K.C. MASTERPIECE® Original Barbecue
    Sauce
  Fresh oregano sprigs
  Grilled mushrooms (optional)

Rinse salmon; pat dry with paper towels. Combine lemon juice and soy sauce in shallow glass dish. Add salmon; let stand at cool room temperature no more than 15 to 20 minutes, turning salmon several times. Remove salmon from marinade; discard marinade. Season lightly with salt and pepper.

Lightly oil hot grid to prevent sticking. Grill salmon on covered grill over medium KINGSFORD® Briquets 10 to 14 minutes. Halfway through cooking time brush salmon with barbecue sauce, then turn and continue grilling until fish flakes easily when tested with fork. Remove fish from grill; brush with barbecue sauce. Garnish with oregano sprigs and mushrooms. *Makes 4 servings*

Blackened Sea Bass

Hardwood charcoal*
2 teaspoons paprika
1 teaspoon garlic salt
1 teaspoon dried thyme
   leaves, crushed
¼ teaspoon ground white
   pepper
¼ teaspoon ground red pepper
¼ teaspoon ground black
   pepper
3 tablespoons butter or
   margarine
4 skinless sea bass or catfish
   fillets (4 to 6 ounces each)
Lemon halves
Fresh dill sprigs for garnish

*Hardwood charcoal takes somewhat longer than regular charcoal to become hot, but results in a hotter fire than regular charcoal. A hot fire is necessary to seal in juices and cook fish quickly. If hardwood charcoal is not available, scatter dry hardwood, mesquite or hickory chunks over hot coals to create a hot fire.

1. Prepare barbecue grill for direct cooking using hardwood charcoal.

2. Meanwhile, combine paprika, garlic salt, thyme and white, red and black peppers in small bowl; mix well. Set aside. Melt butter in small saucepan over medium heat. Pour melted butter into pie plate or shallow bowl. Cool slightly.

3. Dip sea bass into melted butter, evenly coating both sides. Sprinkle both sides of sea bass evenly with paprika mixture.

4. Place sea bass on grid. (Fire will flare up when sea bass is placed on grid, but will subside when grill is covered.) Grill sea bass, on covered grill, over hot coals 4 to 6 minutes or until sea bass is blackened and flakes easily when tested with fork, turning halfway through grilling time. Serve with lemon halves. Garnish, if desired.   *Makes 4 servings*

Note: A lean to moderately fatty saltwater fish, sea bass is generally available year-round. And don't worry about the salt! Saltwater fish are quite low in sodium—they have a special structure that prevents them from becoming as salty as the sea.

Blackened Sea Bass

Grilled Fish with Orange-Chile Salsa

3 medium oranges, peeled and sectioned* (about 1¼ cups segments)
¼ cup finely diced green, red or yellow bell pepper
3 tablespoons chopped cilantro, divided
3 tablespoons lime juice, divided
1 tablespoon honey
1 teaspoon minced, seeded serrano pepper or 1 tablespoon minced jalapeño pepper
1¼ pounds firm white fish fillets, such as orange roughy, lingcod, halibut or red snapper
Lime slices
Zucchini ribbons, cooked

*Canned mandarin orange segments can be substituted for fresh orange segments, if desired.

To prepare Orange-Chile Salsa, combine orange segments, bell pepper, 2 tablespoons cilantro, 2 tablespoons lime juice, honey and serrano pepper. Set aside.

Season fish fillets with remaining 1 tablespoon cilantro and 1 tablespoon lime juice. Lightly oil grid to prevent sticking. Grill fish on covered grill over medium KINGSFORD® Briquets 5 minutes. Turn and top with lime slices, if desired. Grill about 5 minutes until fish flakes easily when tested with fork. Serve with Orange-Chile Salsa. Garnish with zucchini ribbons.

Makes 4 servings

Note: Allow about 10 minutes grilling time per inch thickness of fish fillets.

Hot Off The Grill

For direct cooking, arrange the coals in a single layer directly under the food. Use this method for quick-cooking foods, such as hamburgers, steaks and fish.

Grilled Fish with Orange-Chile Salsa

Sweet Citrus and Dijon Grilled Shrimp

½ cup **LAWRY'S®** Dijon & Honey Marinade with Lemon Juice
½ cup orange juice
½ teaspoon **LAWRY'S®** Garlic Salt
1 pound raw large shrimp, peeled and deveined
1 onion, cut into wedges
8 cherry tomatoes
2 limes, cut into wedges

In medium bowl, combine Dijon & Honey Marinade, orange juice and Garlic Salt; mix well. Arrange shrimp, onion, tomatoes and limes in well-oiled wire grill basket; brush with marinade mixture. Grill 4 to 6 minutes or until shrimp are pink, turning once and basting often with marinade mixture. *Makes 4 servings*

Serving Suggestion: Serve with hot cooked orzo. Garnish with fresh thyme, if desired.

Lemon Tarragon Fish

½ cup **CRISCO®** Oil
1 teaspoon grated lemon peel (optional)
½ cup lemon juice
2 teaspoons dried parsley flakes
2 teaspoons dried tarragon leaves
¼ teaspoon salt
⅛ teaspoon pepper
4 cod, halibut or haddock steaks (about 1 pound)
2⅔ cups hot cooked rice (cooked without salt or fat)

1. Combine oil, lemon peel, if desired, lemon juice, parsley, tarragon, salt and pepper in shallow baking dish. Stir to mix well.

2. Place fish in lemon juice mixture. Turn to coat. Refrigerate 30 minutes, turning after 15 minutes.

3. Prepare grill or heat broiler.

4. Remove fish from marinade; discard marinade. Grill or broil 3 to 5 minutes per side or until fish flakes easily with fork. Serve with hot rice. *Makes 4 servings*

Sweet Citrus and Dijon Grilled Shrimp

Grilled Salmon Quesadillas with Cucumber Salsa

1 medium cucumber, peeled, seeded and finely chopped
½ cup green or red salsa
1 (8-ounce) salmon fillet
3 tablespoons olive oil, divided
4 (10-inch) flour tortillas, warmed
6 ounces goat cheese, crumbled or 1½ cups (6 ounces) shredded Monterey Jack cheese
¼ cup drained sliced pickled jalapeño peppers

1. Prepare grill for direct cooking. Combine cucumber and salsa in small bowl; set aside.

2. Brush salmon with 2 tablespoons oil. Grill, covered, over medium-hot coals 5 to 6 minutes per side or until fish flakes easily when tested with fork. Transfer to plate; flake with fork.

3. Spoon salmon evenly over half of each tortilla, leaving 1-inch border. Sprinkle with cheese and jalapeño slices. Fold tortillas in half. Brush tortillas with remaining 1 tablespoon oil.

4. Grill quesadillas over medium-hot coals until browned on both sides and cheese is melted. Serve with cucumber salsa.

Makes 4 servings

Prep and Cook Time: *20 minutes*

Garlic Skewered Shrimp

1 pound large shrimp, peeled and deveined
2 tablespoons low-sodium soy sauce
1 tablespoon vegetable oil
3 cloves garlic, minced
¼ teaspoon crushed red pepper flakes (optional)
3 green onions, cut into 1-inch pieces

Prepare grill or preheat broiler. Soak 4 (12-inch) wooden skewers in water 20 minutes. Meanwhile, place shrimp in large plastic bag. Combine soy sauce, oil, garlic and pepper in cup; mix well. Pour over shrimp. Close bag securely; turn to coat. Marinate at room temperature 15 minutes.

Drain shrimp; reserve marinade. Alternately thread shrimp and onions onto skewers. Place skewers on grid or rack of broiler pan. Brush with reserved marinade; discard any remaining marinade. Grill, covered, over medium-hot coals or broil 5 to 6 inches from heat 5 minutes on each side or until shrimp are pink and opaque. Serve on lettuce-lined plate.

Makes 4 servings

Tip: For a prettier presentation, leave the tails on the shrimp.

Grilled Salmon Quesadilla with Cucumber Salsa

Grilled Swordfish á l'Orange

4 swordfish, halibut or shark steaks (about 1½ pounds)
1 orange
¾ cup orange juice
1 tablespoon lemon juice
1 tablespoon sesame oil
1 tablespoon soy sauce
1 teaspoon cornstarch
Salt and black pepper to taste

Rinse swordfish and pat dry with paper towels. Grate enough orange peel to measure 1 teaspoon; set aside. Peel orange and cut into sections; set aside. Combine orange juice, lemon juice, oil and soy sauce in small bowl. Pour half of orange juice mixture into shallow glass dish. Add ½ teaspoon grated orange peel to orange juice mixture. Place fish in dish; turn to coat in mixture. Cover and allow to marinate in refrigerator for at least 1 hour.

Place remaining half of orange juice mixture in small saucepan. Stir in cornstarch and remaining ½ teaspoon orange peel. Heat over medium-high heat, stirring constantly, 3 to 5 minutes or until sauce thickens; set aside.

Remove fish from marinade; discard remaining marinade. Lightly sprinkle fish with salt and pepper. Grill over medium coals 3 to 4 minutes per side or until fish is opaque and flakes easily when tested with fork. Top with reserved orange sections and orange sauce. Serve immediately.   *Makes 4 servings*

A.1.® Grilled Fish Steaks

1 pound salmon steaks or other fish steaks, about 1 inch thick
¼ cup A.1.® Steak Sauce
1 tablespoon PARKAY® 70% Vegetable Oil Spread, melted
½ teaspoon garlic powder

Coat large sheet of aluminum foil with non stick cooking spray; place fish steaks on foil. In small bowl, combine steak sauce, spread and garlic powder; spoon over fish. Fold edges of foil together to seal; place seam side up on grill. Grill for about 10 minutes or until fish flakes easily when tested with fork. Carefully remove from grill. Serve immediately.   *Makes 4 servings*

Grilled Swordfish á l'Orange

Seafood Kabobs

Nonstick cooking spray
1 pound raw large shrimp, peeled, deveined
10 ounces skinless swordfish or halibut steaks, cut 1 inch thick
2 tablespoons honey mustard
2 teaspoons fresh lemon juice
8 metal skewers (12 inches long)
8 slices bacon (regular slice, not thick)
Lemon wedges (optional)

1. Spray room temperature barbecue grid with nonstick cooking spray. Prepare barbecue grill for direct cooking.

2. Place shrimp in shallow glass dish. Cut swordfish into 1-inch cubes on cutting board; add to shrimp in dish.

3. Combine honey mustard and lemon juice in small bowl. Pour over shrimp mixture; toss lightly to coat.

4. To assemble skewers, pierce skewer through 1 end of bacon slice. Add 1 piece shrimp. Pierce skewer through bacon slice again, wrapping bacon slice around 1 side of shrimp.

5. Add 1 piece swordfish. Pierce bacon slice again, wrapping bacon around opposite side of swordfish. Continue adding seafood and wrapping with bacon, pushing ingredients to middle of skewer until end of bacon slice is reached. Repeat with remaining skewers. Brush any remaining mustard mixture over skewers.

6. Place skewers on grid. Grill skewers, on covered grill, over medium coals 8 to 10 minutes or until shrimp are opaque and swordfish flakes easily when tested with fork, turning halfway through grilling time. Serve with lemon wedges.

Makes 4 servings (2 kabobs per serving)

Note: Kabobs can be prepared up to 3 hours before grilling. Cover and refrigerate until ready to grill.

Seafood Kabobs

Mediterranean Grilled Snapper

1 whole red snapper (about 4½ pounds), scaled, gutted and cavity cut open*
2 tablespoons fresh lemon juice
Salt and pepper
3 tablespoons olive oil, divided
2 tablespoons chopped fresh oregano leaves *or* 2 teaspoons dried oregano leaves, crushed
2 tablespoons chopped fresh basil leaves *or* 2 teaspoons dried basil leaves, crushed
4 slices lemon
1 metal skewer (6 inches long)
3 whole heads garlic**
Hinged fish basket (optional)
Fresh oregano sprigs (optional)
6 slices Italian bread, cut 1 inch thick
Additional olive oil (optional)

*This can be done by your fish retailer at the time of purchase or you may wish to do this yourself.

**The whole garlic bulb is called a head.

1. Prepare barbecue grill for direct cooking. Rinse snapper under cold running water; pat dry with paper towels. Open cavity of snapper; brush with lemon juice. Sprinkle lightly with salt and pepper. Combine 1 tablespoon oil, chopped oregano and basil in small bowl. Using small spatula, spread mixture inside cavity of snapper. Place lemon slices in cavity; close snapper. Secure opening by threading skewer lengthwise through outside edge of cavity.

2. Cut off top third of garlic heads to expose cloves; discard. Place each head on small sheet of heavy-duty foil; drizzle evenly with remaining 2 tablespoons oil. Wrap in foil. Place packets directly on medium-hot coals.

3. Place snapper in oiled, hinged fish basket or directly on oiled grid. Grill snapper and garlic, on uncovered grill, over medium-hot coals 20 to 25 minutes or until snapper flakes easily when tested with fork, turning halfway through grilling time.

4. Soak oregano sprigs in water. Place oregano sprigs directly on coals during last 10 minutes of grilling.

5. Brush bread lightly with additional oil. During last 5 minutes of grilling, place bread around outer edges of grid to toast, about 4 minutes, turning once.

6. Transfer snapper to carving board. Carefully unwrap garlic. Peel off any charred papery outer skin. Using pot holder, squeeze softened garlic from heads into small bowl; mash to a paste with wooden spoon or potato masher, adding additional oil. Spread bread lightly with garlic paste.

7. Remove skewer from snapper. Slit skin from head to tail along back and belly of snapper; pull skin from top side of snapper with fingers. Discard skin. Using utility knife, separate top fillet from backbone; cut into serving-size pieces. Lift up tail; pull forward to free backbone from lower fillet. Cut lower fillet into serving-size pieces. Remove skin, if desired. *Makes 6 servings*

Mediterranean Grilled Snapper

Tandoori-Style Seafood Kabobs

½ pound each salmon fillet,
    tuna steak and swordfish
    steak*
1 teaspoon salt
1 teaspoon ground cumin
¼ teaspoon black pepper
    Dash ground cinnamon
    Dash ground cloves
    Dash ground nutmeg
    Dash ground cardamom
    (optional)
½ cup plain low-fat yogurt
¼ cup lemon juice
1 piece (1-inch cube) peeled
    fresh ginger, minced
1 tablespoon olive oil
2 cloves garlic, minced
½ jalapeño pepper, seeded and
    minced
½ pound large shrimp, shelled
    with tails intact, deveined
1 each red and green bell
    pepper, cut into bite-size
    pieces
    Fresh parsley sprigs
    Fresh chives

*Any firm fish can be substituted for any fish listed above.

Cut fish into 1½-inch cubes; cover and refrigerate. Heat salt and spices in small skillet over medium heat until fragrant (or spices may be added to marinade without heating); place spices in 2-quart glass dish. Add yogurt, lemon juice, ginger, oil, garlic and jalapeño pepper; mix well. Add fish and shrimp; turn to coat. Cover and refrigerate at least 1 hour but no longer than 2 hours. Thread a variety of seafood onto each metal or wooden skewer, alternating with bell peppers. (Soak wooden skewers in hot water 30 minutes to prevent burning.) Grill kabobs over medium-hot KINGSFORD® Briquets about 2 minutes per side until fish flakes easily when tested with fork and shrimp are pink and opaque. Remove seafood and peppers from skewers. Garnish with parsley and chives. *Makes 4 servings*

Hot Off The Grill

Spray skewers with nonstick cooking spray before threading ingredients onto the skewers. This will make removing the grilled food a snap.

Tandoori-Style Seafood Kabobs

Grilled Swordfish with Hot Red Sauce

2 to 3 green onions
**4 swordfish or halibut steaks
(about 1½ pounds total)**
2 tablespoons hot bean paste*
2 tablespoons soy sauce
**2 tablespoons Sesame Salt
(recipe follows)**
1 tablespoon dark sesame oil
4 teaspoons sugar
4 cloves garlic, minced
⅛ teaspoon pepper

Available in specialty stores or Asian markets.

1. Spray grid of barbecue grill or broiler rack with nonstick cooking spray. Prepare coals for grill or preheat broiler.

2. Cut off and discard root ends of green onions. Finely chop enough green onions to measure ¼ cup; set aside.

3. Rinse swordfish and pat dry with paper towels. Place in shallow glass dish.

4. Combine green onions, hot bean paste, soy sauce, Sesame Salt, sesame oil, sugar, garlic and pepper in small bowl; mix well.

5. Spread half of marinade over fish; turn fish over and spread with remaining marinade. Cover with plastic wrap and refrigerate 30 minutes.

6. Remove fish from marinade; discard remaining marinade. Place fish on prepared grid. Grill fish over medium-hot coals or broil 4 to 5 minutes per side or until fish is opaque and flakes easily with fork. Garnish as desired. *Makes 4 servings*

Sesame Salt
½ cup sesame seeds
¼ teaspoon salt

To toast sesame seeds, heat small skillet over medium heat. Add sesame seeds; cook and stir about 5 minutes or until seeds are golden. Cool. Crush toasted sesame seeds and salt with mortar and pestle or process in clean coffee or spice grinder. Refrigerate in covered glass jar.

Grilled Swordfish with Hot Red Sauce

Trout Stuffed with Fresh Mint and Oranges

**2 pan-dressed* trout (1 to
   1¼ pounds each)
½ teaspoon coarse salt, such as
   Kosher salt
1 orange, sliced
1 cup fresh mint leaves
1 sweet onion, sliced**

*A pan-dressed trout has been gutted and scaled with head and tail removed.

1. Rinse trout under cold running water; pat dry with paper towels.

2. Sprinkle cavities of trout with salt; fill each with orange slices and mint. Cover each fish with onion slices.

3. Spray 2 large sheets of foil with nonstick cooking spray. Place 1 fish on each sheet and seal using Drugstore Wrap technique.**

4. Place foil packets seam-side down directly on medium-hot coals; grill on covered grill 20 to 25 minutes or until trout flakes easily when tested with fork, turning once.

5. Carefully open foil packets; remove and discard orange-mint stuffing and trout skin. Serve immediately.   *Makes 6 servings*

**Place food in the center of an oblong piece of heavy-duty foil, leaving at least a two-inch border around the food. Bring the two long sides together above the food; fold down in a series of locked folds, allowing for heat circulation and expansion. Fold short ends up and over again. Press folds firmly to seal the foil packet.

Fish in Foil

**1 (8-ounce) can stewed
   tomatoes
⅓ cup A.1.® Bold & Spicy Steak
   Sauce
1 clove garlic, minced
4 (4-ounce) firm fish fillets
2 cups frozen mixed
   vegetables**

In small bowl, combine stewed tomatoes, steak sauce and garlic; set aside.

Place each fish fillet in center of heavy duty or double thickness foil; top each with ½ cup mixed vegetables and ¼ cup steak sauce mixture. Wrap foil securely.

Grill fish packets over medium heat 8 to 10 minutes or until fish flakes easily with fork. Serve immediately.   *Makes 4 servings*

Trout Stuffed with Fresh Mint and Oranges

Curried Apricot Glazed Shrimp and Beef

½ cup **A.1.® Thick & Hearty Steak Sauce**
⅓ cup **apricot preserves**
2 teaspoons **curry powder**
2 cloves **garlic, minced**
1 pound **large shrimp, peeled, deveined**
1 (1-pound) **beef top round steak, cut into 1-inch cubes**
1 cup **snow peas, cut in half**
Hot cooked couscous

Soak 8 (10-inch) wooden skewers in water at least 30 minutes.

In small bowl, combine steak sauce, preserves, curry and garlic. Place shrimp and steak in nonmetal dish; coat with ½ cup steak sauce mixture. Cover; refrigerate 2 hours, stirring occasionally.

Remove shrimp and steak from marinade; discard marinade. Alternately thread shrimp, beef and snow peas onto wooden or metal skewers. Grill kabobs over medium heat or broil 6 inches from heat source 5 minutes on each side or until steak is desired doneness and shrimp turn opaque, basting with remaining steak sauce mixture. Serve immediately with couscous. Garnish as desired.

Makes 4 servings

Szechuan Tuna Steaks

4 **tuna steaks (6 ounces each), cut 1 inch thick**
¼ cup **soy sauce**
¼ cup **dry sherry or sake**
1 tablespoon **dark sesame oil**
1 teaspoon **hot chili oil** *or* ¼ teaspoon **crushed red pepper**
1 clove **garlic, minced**
3 tablespoons **chopped fresh cilantro**

Place tuna in single layer in large shallow glass dish. Combine soy sauce, sherry, sesame oil, hot chili oil and garlic in small bowl. Reserve ¼ cup soy sauce mixture at room temperature. Pour remaining soy sauce mixture over tuna. Cover and marinate in refrigerator 40 minutes, turning once.

Prepare grill. Drain tuna, discarding marinade. Place tuna on grid. Grill, uncovered, over medium-hot coals 6 minutes or until tuna is opaque, but still feels somewhat soft in center,* turning halfway through grilling time. Transfer tuna to carving board. Cut each tuna steak into thin slices; fan out slices onto serving plates. Drizzle tuna slices with reserved soy sauce mixture; sprinkle with cilantro.

Makes 4 servings

*Tuna becomes dry and tough if overcooked. Cook it as if it were beef.

Curried Apricot Glazed Shrimp and Beef

Lobster Tails with Tasty Butters

**Hot & Spicy Butter or
Scallion Butter or Chili-
Mustard Butter
(recipes follow)
4 fresh or thawed frozen
lobster tails (about
5 ounces each)**

Prepare grill for direct cooking. Prepare 1 butter mixture.

Rinse lobster tails in cold water. Butterfly tails by cutting lengthwise through centers of hard top shells and meat. Cut to, but not through, bottoms of shells. Press shell halves of tails apart with fingers. Brush lobster meat with butter mixture.

Place tails on grid, meat side down. Grill over medium-high heat 4 minutes. Turn tails meat side up. Brush with butter mixture and grill 4 to 5 minutes or until lobster meat turns opaque.

Heat remaining butter mixture, stirring occasionally. Serve butter sauce for dipping. *Makes 4 servings*

Tasty Butters

Hot & Spicy Butter
 1/3 **cup butter or margarine, melted**
 1 **tablespoon chopped onion**
 1 **teaspoon dried thyme leaves**
 1/4 **teaspoon ground allspice**
 2 **to 3 teaspoons hot pepper sauce**

Scallion Butter
 1/3 **cup butter or margarine, melted**
 1 **tablespoon finely chopped green onion tops**
 1 **tablespoon lemon juice**
 1 **teaspoon grated lemon peel**
 1/4 **teaspoon black pepper**

Chili-Mustard Butter
 1/3 **cup butter or margarine, melted**
 1 **tablespoon chopped onion**
 1 **tablespoon Dijon mustard**
 1 **teaspoon chili powder**

For each butter sauce, combine ingredients in small bowl.

Lobster Tail with Tasty Butter

Salmon with Fresh Pineapple Salsa

1 cup plus 1½ tablespoons LAWRY'S® Teriyaki Marinade with Pineapple Juice, divided
1¼ pounds fresh salmon fillets or steaks
1 cup chopped fresh or canned pineapple, drained
¼ cup finely chopped red onion
2 tablespoons chopped red bell pepper
1 tablespoon chopped fresh cilantro
1 tablespoon minced fresh jalapeño chile pepper*

*Jalapeño peppers can sting and irritate the skin; wear rubber gloves when handling and do not touch eyes.

In large resealable plastic food storage bag, combine 1 cup Teriyaki Marinade and salmon; seal bag. Marinate in refrigerator at least 30 minutes. In small bowl, combine pineapple, onion, bell pepper, additional 1½ tablespoons Teriyaki Marinade, cilantro and jalapeño; mix gently. Let stand at room temperature 30 minutes to allow flavors to blend. Remove salmon; discard used marinade. Grill or broil salmon 10 to 12 minutes or until fish flakes easily when tested with fork, turning halfway through grilling time. Top with pineapple salsa.

Makes 4 servings

Serving Suggestion: Serve with herbed rice pilaf and sugar snap peas.

Hot Off The Grill

Wash all utensils, cutting boards and containers with hot soapy water after they have been in contact with uncooked meat.

Salmon with Fresh Pineapple Salsa

Beach Grill

1 cup vegetable oil
2 teaspoons LAWRY'S®
    Seasoned Salt
1 teaspoon LAWRY'S® Garlic
    Powder with Parsley
½ teaspoon hot pepper sauce
    (optional)
12 raw medium shrimp, peeled
    and deveined
12 sea scallops
1 small red onion, cut into
    12 wedges

In large resealable plastic food storage bag, combine oil, Seasoned Salt, Garlic Powder with Parsley and hot pepper sauce, if desired; mix well. Add shrimp, scallops and onion; seal bag. Marinate in refrigerator at least 1 hour. Remove shrimp, scallops and onion; discard used marinade. Alternately thread shrimp, scallops and onion onto skewers. Grill or broil skewers 4 to 6 minutes or until shrimp are pink and scallops are opaque, turning halfway through grilling time.   *Makes 6 servings*

Serving Suggestion: Serve with lime wedges and crusty French bread.

Tuna Vera Cruz

3 tablespoons tequila, rum or
    vodka
2 tablespoons lime juice
2 teaspoons grated lime peel
1 piece (1-inch cube) fresh
    ginger, minced
2 cloves garlic, minced
1 teaspoon salt
1 teaspoon sugar
½ teaspoon ground cumin
¼ teaspoon ground cinnamon
¼ teaspoon black pepper
1 tablespoon vegetable oil
1½ pounds fresh tuna, halibut,
    swordfish or shark steaks
    Lemon and lime wedges
    Fresh rosemary sprigs

Combine tequila, lime juice, lime peel, ginger, garlic, salt, sugar, cumin, cinnamon and pepper in 2-quart glass dish; stir in oil. Add tuna; turn to coat. Cover and refrigerate at least 30 minutes. Remove tuna from marinade; discard marinade. Grill tuna over medium-hot KINGSFORD® Briquets about 4 minutes per side until fish flakes easily when tested with fork. Garnish with lemon wedges, lime wedges and rosemary sprigs.   *Makes 4 servings*

Beach Grill

Shanghai Fish Packets

4 orange roughy or tilefish fillets (4 to 6 ounces each)
¼ cup mirin* or Rhine wine
3 tablespoons soy sauce
1 tablespoon dark sesame oil
1½ teaspoons grated fresh ginger
¼ teaspoon crushed red pepper
1 tablespoon peanut or vegetable oil
1 clove garlic, minced
1 package (10 ounces) fresh spinach leaves, destemmed

*Mirin is a Japanese sweet wine available in Japanese markets and the gourmet section of large supermarkets.

1. Prepare barbecue grill for direct cooking.

2. Place orange roughy in single layer in large shallow dish. Combine mirin, soy sauce, sesame oil, ginger and crushed red pepper in small bowl; pour over orange roughy. Cover; marinate in refrigerator 20 minutes.

3. Heat peanut oil in large skillet over medium heat. Add garlic; cook and stir 1 minute. Add spinach; cook and stir until wilted, about 3 minutes, tossing with 2 wooden spoons.

4. Place spinach mixture in center of four 12-inch squares of heavy-duty foil. Remove orange roughy from marinade; reserve marinade. Place 1 orange roughy fillet over each mound of spinach. Drizzle reserved marinade evenly over orange roughy. Wrap in foil.

5. Place packets on grid. Grill packets, on covered grill, over medium coals 15 to 18 minutes or until orange roughy flakes easily when tested with fork.

Makes 4 servings

Grilled Fresh Fish

3 to 3½ pounds fresh tuna or catfish
¾ cup prepared HIDDEN VALLEY® Original Ranch® Salad Dressing
Chopped fresh dill
Lemon wedges (optional)

Place fish on heavy-duty foil. Cover with salad dressing. Grill over medium-hot coals until fish turns opaque and flakes easily when tested with fork, 20 to 30 minutes. Or broil fish 15 to 20 minutes. Sprinkle with dill; garnish with lemon wedges, if desired.

Makes 6 servings

Shanghai Fish Packet

Tuna Kabobs with Red Pepper Relish

1 pound tuna steak, cut into 1-inch squares
6 tablespoons red pepper jelly*
⅓ cup FRENCH'S® Deli Brown Mustard
2 tablespoons balsamic or red wine vinegar
½ teaspoon cracked black pepper
¼ teaspoon salt
1 red bell pepper, minced
1 green onion, minced
1 orange, unpeeled, cut into 1-inch pieces
1 green bell pepper, cut into 1-inch pieces

*If red pepper jelly is unavailable, combine 6 tablespoons melted apple jelly with 1 tablespoon FRANK'S® Original REDHOT® Cayenne Pepper Sauce. Mix well.

1. Place tuna in large resealable plastic food storage bag. Combine jelly, mustard, vinegar, black pepper and salt in 1-cup measure. Pour ½ cup jelly marinade over tuna. Seal bag; marinate in refrigerator 15 minutes.

2. Combine remaining jelly marinade, red bell pepper and onion in small serving bowl. Reserve for relish.

3. Alternately thread tuna, orange and green bell pepper onto 4 (12-inch) metal skewers. Place skewers on oiled grid. Grill over medium-low heat 8 to 10 minutes or until fish is opaque, but slightly soft in center, turning and basting halfway with marinade.** Serve with red pepper relish.   *Makes 4 servings*

**Tuna becomes dry and tough if overcooked. Watch carefully while grilling.

Prep Time: *25 minutes*
Marinate Time: *15 minutes*
Cook Time: *8 minutes*

Hot Off The Grill

Charcoal lighter fluid can assist in starting a fire and imports no flavor to the cooking food since it burns away within a few minutes after the fire is lit.

Tuna Kabobs with Red Pepper Relish

Seafood Tacos with Fruit Salsa

2 tablespoons lemon juice
1 teaspoon chili powder
1 teaspoon ground allspice
1 teaspoon olive oil
1 teaspoon minced garlic
1 to 2 teaspoons grated lemon peel
½ teaspoon ground cloves
1 pound halibut or snapper fillets
12 (6-inch) corn tortillas or 6 (7- to 8-inch) flour tortillas
3 cups shredded romaine lettuce
1 small red onion, halved and thinly sliced
Fruit Salsa (recipe follows)

1. Combine lemon juice, chili powder, allspice, oil, garlic, lemon peel and cloves in small bowl. Rub fish with spice mixture; cover and refrigerate while grill heats, or refrigerate up to several hours. (Fish may be cut into smaller pieces for easier handling.)

2. Spray grid with nonstick cooking spray. Adjust grid 4 to 6 inches above heat. Preheat grill to medium-high heat. Grill fish, covered, 3 minutes or until fish is lightly seared on bottom. Carefully turn fish over; grill 2 minutes or until fish is opaque in center and flakes easily when tested with fork. Remove from heat and cut into 12 pieces, removing bones if necessary. Cover to keep warm.

3. Place tortillas on grill in single layer and cook 5 to 10 seconds; turn over and cook another 5 to 10 seconds or until hot and pliable. Stack; cover to keep warm.

4. Top each tortilla with ¼ cup lettuce and red onion. Add 1 piece of fish and about 2 tablespoons Fruit Salsa. *Makes 6 servings*

Fruit Salsa

1 small ripe papaya, peeled, seeded and diced
1 firm small banana, diced
2 green onions, minced
3 tablespoons chopped fresh cilantro or mint
3 tablespoons lime juice
2 jalapeño peppers, seeded and minced*

*Jalapeño peppers can sting and irritate the skin; wear rubber gloves when handling peppers and do not touch eyes. Wash hands after handling.

1. Combine all ingredients in small bowl. Serve at room temperature. *Makes 12 servings*

Seafood Tacos with Fruit Salsa

Teriyaki Trout

**4 whole trout (about
    2 pounds)**
**¾ cup LAWRY'S® Teriyaki
    Marinade with Pineapple
    Juice**
½ cup sliced green onions
**2 medium lemons, sliced
    Chopped fresh parsley
    (optional)**

Pierce skin of trout several times with fork. Brush the inside and outside of each trout with Teriyaki Marinade with Pineapple Juice; stuff with green onions and lemon slices. Place in shallow glass dish. Remove ¼ cup Teriyaki Marinade with Pineapple Juice for basting. Pour ½ cup Teriyaki Marinade with Pineapple Juice over trout; cover dish. Marinate in refrigerator at least 30 minutes. Heat grill for medium-hot coals. Remove trout. Place trout in oiled hinged wire grill basket; brush with reserved ¼ cup Teriyaki Marinade with Pineapple Juice. Grill, 4 to 5 inches from heat source, 10 minutes or until trout flakes easily with fork, turning and brushing occasionally with reserved marinade. Do not baste during last 5 minutes of cooking. Discard used marinade. Sprinkle with parsley, if desired. *Makes 4 servings*

Serving Suggestion: For a delicious side dish, cook sliced bell pepper, onion and zucchini brushed with vegetable oil on grill with trout.

Moroccan Swordfish

**4 swordfish steaks (4 ounces
    each), about 1 inch thick**
1 tablespoon lemon juice
**1 tablespoon apple cider
    vinegar**
**2½ teaspoons garlic-flavored
    vegetable oil**
1 teaspoon ground ginger
1 teaspoon paprika
½ teaspoon ground cumin
½ teaspoon hot chili oil
¼ teaspoon salt
¼ teaspoon ground coriander
⅛ teaspoon black pepper
2⅔ cups prepared couscous

1. Place swordfish in single layer in medium shallow dish. Combine lemon juice, vinegar, garlic-flavored oil, ginger, paprika, cumin, chili oil, salt, coriander and pepper in small bowl; pour over swordfish and turn to coat both sides. Cover and refrigerate 40 minutes, turning once.

2. Discard marinade; grill swordfish on uncovered grill over medium-hot coals 8 to 10 minutes or until swordfish is opaque and flakes easily when tested with fork, turning once. Serve with couscous. *Makes 4 servings*

Teriyaki Trout

Cajun Grilled Shrimp

3 green onions, minced
2 tablespoons lemon juice
3 cloves garlic, minced
2 teaspoons paprika
1 teaspoon salt
1/4 to 1/2 teaspoon black pepper
1/4 to 1/2 teaspoon cayenne
    pepper
1 tablespoon olive oil
1 1/2 pounds shrimp, shelled with
    tails intact, deveined
    Lemon wedges

Combine onions, lemon juice, garlic, paprika, salt and peppers in 2-quart glass dish; stir in oil. Add shrimp; turn to coat. Cover and refrigerate at least 15 minutes. Thread shrimp onto metal or wooden skewers. (Soak wooden skewers in hot water 30 minutes to prevent burning.) Grill shrimp over medium-hot KINGSFORD® Briquets about 2 minutes per side until opaque. Serve immediately with lemon wedges.

Makes 4 servings

Grilled Salmon Fillets, Asparagus and Onions

1/2 teaspoon paprika, preferably
    sweet Hungarian
6 salmon fillets (6 to 8 ounces
    each)
1/3 cup bottled honey-Dijon
    marinade or barbecue
    sauce
1 bunch (about 1 pound) fresh
    asparagus spears, ends
    trimmed
1 large red or sweet onion, cut
    into 1/4-inch slices
1 tablespoon olive oil

1. Prepare grill for grilling. Sprinkle paprika evenly over salmon fillets. Brush marinade over salmon; let stand at room temperature 15 minutes.

2. Brush asparagus and onion slices with olive oil; season with salt and pepper.

3. Place salmon, skin side down, in center of grid over medium coals. Arrange asparagus spears and onion slices around salmon on grid. Grill salmon and vegetables over covered grill 5 minutes. Turn asparagus and onion slices. Grill 5 to 6 minutes more or until salmon flakes easily when tested with a fork and vegetables are crisp-tender. Separate onion slices into rings; arrange over asparagus.

Makes 6 servings

Prep and Cook Time: *26 minutes*

Cajun Grilled Shrimp

Snapper with Pesto Butter

½ cup butter or margarine,
    softened
1 cup packed fresh basil
    leaves, coarsely chopped
    or ½ cup chopped fresh
    parsley plus 2 tablespoons
    dried basil leaves, crushed
3 tablespoons finely grated
    fresh Parmesan cheese
1 clove garlic, minced
    Olive oil
2 to 3 teaspoons lemon juice
4 to 6 red snapper, rock cod,
    salmon or other medium-
    firm fish fillets (at least
    ½ inch thick)
    Salt and black pepper
    Lemon wedges
    Fresh basil or parsley sprigs
    and lemon strips for
    garnish

To make Pesto Butter, place butter, basil, cheese, garlic and 1 tablespoon oil in blender or food processor; process until blended. Stir in lemon juice to taste. Rinse fish; pat dry with paper towels. Brush one side of fish lightly with oil; season with salt and pepper.

Oil hot grid to help prevent sticking. Grill fillets, oil sides down, on a covered grill, over medium KINGSFORD® Briquets, 5 to 9 minutes. Halfway through cooking time, brush tops with oil; season with salt and pepper. Turn and continue grilling until fish turns opaque throughout. (Allow 3 to 5 minutes for each ½ inch of thickness.) Serve each fillet with a spoonful of Pesto Butter and a wedge of lemon. Garnish with basil sprigs and lemon strips.

Makes 4 to 6 servings

Hot Off The Grill

Do not use water to quench flare-ups on a gas grill. Simply close the hood and turn down the heat until the flames subside.

Snapper with Pesto Butter

Catfish with Fresh Corn Relish

**4 catfish fillets (each about
  6 ounces and at least ½
  inch thick)**
2 tablespoons paprika
½ teaspoon ground red pepper
½ teaspoon salt
  **Fresh Corn Relish (recipe
  follows)**
  Lime wedges
  Tarragon sprigs for garnish

Rinse fish; pat dry with paper towels. Combine paprika, red pepper and salt in cup; lightly sprinkle on both sides of fish.

Oil hot grid to help prevent sticking. Grill fish, on a covered grill, over medium KINGSFORD® Briquets, 5 to 9 minutes. Halfway through cooking time, turn fish over and continue grilling until fish turns from translucent to opaque throughout. (Grilling time depends on the thickness of fish; allow 3 to 5 minutes for each ½ inch of thickness.) Serve with Fresh Corn Relish and lime wedges. Garnish with tarragon sprigs.   *Makes 4 servings*

Fresh Corn Relish
  ¼ cup cooked fresh corn or thawed frozen corn
  ¼ cup finely diced green bell pepper
  ¼ cup finely slivered red onion
  1 tablespoon vegetable oil
  2 tablespoons seasoned (sweet) rice vinegar
    Salt and black pepper
  ½ cup cherry tomatoes, cut into quarters

Toss together corn, green pepper, onion, oil and vinegar in medium bowl. Season with salt and pepper. Cover and refrigerate until ready to serve. Just before serving, gently mix in tomatoes.
Makes about 1½ cups

Catfish with Fresh Corn Relish

Grilled Prawns with Salsa Vera Cruz

1 can (14½ ounces)
     **DEL MONTE® Mexican
     Recipe Stewed Tomatoes,
     drained and chopped**
1 **orange, peeled and chopped**
¼ **cup sliced green onions**
¼ **cup chopped cilantro or
     parsley**
1 **small clove garlic, crushed**
1 **pound medium shrimp,
     peeled and deveined**

1. Combine tomatoes, orange, green onions, cilantro and garlic in medium bowl.

2. Thread shrimp onto skewers; season with salt and pepper, if desired.

3. Brush grill with oil. Cook shrimp over hot coals about 3 minutes on each side or until shrimp turn pink. Top with salsa. Serve over rice and garnish, if desired.   *Makes 4 servings*

Hint: Thoroughly rinse shrimp in cold water before cooking.

Prep Time: *25 minutes*
Cook Time: *6 minutes*

Grilled Tuna with Salsa Salad

1 bag (16 ounces) **BIRDS EYE®
     frozen Farm Fresh
     Mixtures Broccoli, Corn &
     Red Peppers**
6 to 8 **green onions, sliced**
1 to 2 **jalapeño peppers, finely
     chopped**
1 can (14½ ounces) **diced
     tomatoes with garlic and
     onion***
1 **tablespoon, or to taste, lime
     juice or vinegar**
4 **tuna steaks, grilled**

*Or, substitute favorite seasoned diced tomatoes.

• In large saucepan, cook vegetables according to package directions; drain.

• In large bowl, combine vegetables, onions, peppers, tomatoes and lime juice. Let stand 15 minutes.

• Serve vegetable mixture over tuna.   *Makes 4 servings*

Prep Time: *5 minutes*
Cook Time: *10 minutes*

Grilled Prawns with Salsa Vera Cruz

Grilled Shrimp Creole

1 can (15 ounces) red beans
½ cup olive oil, divided
3 tablespoons balsamic or red
    wine vinegar
3 cloves garlic, minced,
    divided
1½ pounds raw large shrimp,
    peeled and deveined
3 tablespoons all-purpose
    flour
1 medium green bell pepper,
    coarsely chopped
1 medium onion, coarsely
    chopped
2 ribs celery, sliced
1 can (28 ounces) tomatoes,
    undrained, coarsely
    chopped
1 bay leaf
½ teaspoons dried thyme
    leaves, crushed
¾ teaspoon hot pepper sauce
1 cup uncooked white rice,
    preferably converted
1 can (about 14 ounces)
    chicken broth
Hinged grill basket or 6
    metal skewers (12 inches
    long)
¼ cup chopped fresh parsley

1. Place beans in strainer. Rinse under cold running water; drain. Set aside.

2. Combine ¼ cup oil, vinegar and 1 clove garlic in small bowl. Pour over shrimp; toss lightly to coat. Cover; marinate in refrigerator at least 30 minutes or up to 8 hours, turning occasionally.

3. For tomato sauce, heat remaining ¼ cup oil in large skillet over medium heat. Stir in flour. Cook and stir until flour is dark golden brown, 10 to 12 minutes. Add bell pepper, onion, celery and remaining 2 cloves garlic; cook and stir 5 minutes. Add tomatoes with juice, bay leaf, thyme and hot pepper sauce. Simmer, uncovered, 25 to 30 minutes or until sauce has thickened and vegetables are fork-tender, stirring occasionally.*

4. Meanwhile, prepare barbecue grill for direct cooking.

5. While coals are heating, prepare rice according to package directions, substituting broth for 1¾ cups water and omitting salt. Stir in beans during last 5 minutes of cooking.

6. Drain shrimp; discard marinade. Place shrimp in grill basket or thread onto skewers. Place grill basket or skewers on grid. Grill shrimp, on uncovered grill, over medium coals 6 to 8 minutes or until shrimp are opaque, turning halfway through grilling time.

7. Remove and discard bay leaf from tomato sauce. Arrange rice and beans on 4 serving plates; top with tomato sauce. Remove shrimp from grill basket or skewers. Arrange shrimp over tomato sauce. Sprinkle with parsley.
Makes 4 servings

If desired, tomato sauce may be prepared up to 1 day ahead. Cover and refrigerate. Reheat sauce in medium saucepan over medium heat while shrimp are grilling.

Grilled Shrimp Creole

Smokin' Sides

Mesquite Summer Vegetable Medley (page 348)

Grilled Cajun Potato Wedges (page 350)

Grilled Tri-Colored Pepper Salad

1 each large red, yellow and green bell pepper,
    cut into halves or quarters
⅓ cup extra-virgin olive oil
3 tablespoons balsamic vinegar
2 cloves garlic, minced
¼ teaspoon salt
¼ teaspoon black pepper
⅓ cup crumbled goat cheese (about 1½ ounces)
¼ cup thinly sliced fresh basil leaves

1. Prepare barbecue grill for direct cooking.

2. Place bell peppers, skin-side down, on grid. Grill bell peppers, on covered grill, over hot coals 10 to 12 minutes or until skin is charred. Place charred bell peppers in paper bag. Close bag; set aside to cool 10 to 15 minutes. Remove skin with paring knife; discard skin.

3. Place bell peppers in shallow glass serving dish. Combine oil, vinegar, garlic, salt and black pepper in small bowl; whisk until well combined. Pour over bell peppers. Let stand 30 minutes at room temperature. (Or, cover and refrigerate up to 24 hours. Bring bell peppers to room temperature before serving.)

4. Sprinkle bell peppers with cheese and basil just before serving.   *Makes 4 to 6 servings*

Grilled Vegetable & Orzo Salad with Citrus Vinaigrette

½ cup thinly sliced shallots or
    green onions
⅓ cup white wine vinegar
¼ cup orange juice
2 tablespoons lemon juice
2 tablespoons extra-virgin
    olive oil
1½ teaspoons grated orange
    peel
1½ teaspoons grated lemon
    peel
1½ teaspoons salt
¼ teaspoon black pepper
10 large mushrooms, cut in half
1 package (10 ounces) frozen
    artichoke hearts, thawed
12 ounces orzo pasta, cooked,
    rinsed and drained
2 red or green bell peppers,
    cut in half, stemmed and
    seeded
12 large fresh basil leaves,
    minced (optional)
Orange peel strips

Combine shallots, vinegar, juices, oil, peels, salt and black pepper in large bowl; whisk until blended. Add mushrooms and artichokes; let stand 30 minutes. Thread artichokes and mushrooms onto wooden skewers; reserve vinaigrette. (Soak wooden skewers in hot water 30 minutes to prevent burning.) Add orzo to reserved dressing; toss to coat. Grill artichokes and mushrooms on covered grill over medium-hot KINGSFORD® Briquets 3 to 5 minutes per side. Grill bell peppers, skin sides down, over medium-hot briquets about 8 minutes until skins on all sides are charred. Place peppers in large resealable plastic food storage bag or paper bag; seal. Let stand 5 minutes; remove skin. Slice mushrooms and chop peppers; add to pasta with artichokes and basil, tossing until coated. Serve at room temperature. Garnish with orange peel strips.

Makes 8 side-dish servings (about 1 cup each)

Hot Off The Grill

To make an entrée that serves four, add 1 can (15 ounces) rinsed and drained black beans or 2 cups cubed grilled chicken or sliced grilled sausage.

Grilled Vegetable & Orzo Salad with Citrus Vinaigrette

Buffalo Chili Onions

½ cup **FRANK'S® Original REDHOT® Cayenne Pepper Sauce**
½ cup **(1 stick) butter or margarine, melted or olive oil**
¼ cup **chili sauce**
1 tablespoon **chili powder**
4 large **sweet onions, cut into ½-inch-thick slices**

Whisk together RedHot® sauce, butter, chili sauce and chili powder in medium bowl until blended; brush on onion slices.

Place onions on grid. Grill over medium-high coals 10 minutes or until tender, turning and basting often with the chili mixture. Serve warm.   *Makes 6 side-dish servings*

Tip: Onions may be prepared ahead and grilled just before serving.

Prep Time: *10 minutes*
Cook Time: *10 minutes*

Jamaican Grilled Sweet Potatoes

2 large **(about 1½ pounds) sweet potatoes or yams**
3 tablespoons **packed brown sugar**
2 tablespoons **softened margarine, divided**
1 teaspoon **ground ginger**
2 teaspoons **dark rum**
1 tablespoon **chopped fresh cilantro**

1. Pierce potatoes in several places with fork. Place on paper towel in microwave. Microwave at HIGH 5 to 6 minutes or until crisp-tender when tested with fork, rotating ¼ turn halfway through cooking. Let stand 10 minutes. Diagonally slice about ½ inch off ends of potatoes. Continue cutting potatoes diagonally into ¾-inch-thick slices.

2. Combine brown sugar, 1 tablespoon margarine and ginger in small bowl; mix well. Stir in rum, then cilantro; set aside.

3. Melt remaining 1 tablespoon margarine. With half of melted margarine, lightly brush one side of each potato slice. Grill slices margarine-side down on covered grill over medium coals 4 to 6 minutes or until grillmarked. Brush tops with remaining melted margarine; turn over and grill 3 to 5 minutes or until grillmarked. To serve, spoon rum mixture equally over potato slices.

Makes 6 servings

Prep and Cook Time: *30 minutes*

Buffalo Chili Onions

Zesty Corn-on-the-Cob

6 ears fresh corn
¼ cup margarine or butter, melted
1 tablespoon chopped fresh parsley
2 teaspoons prepared horseradish
¼ teaspoon paprika
¼ teaspoon black pepper
⅛ teaspoon salt

Pull outer husks from top to base of each corn ear; leave husks attached to ear. Strip away silk. Trim any blemishes from corn. Place corn in large bowl. Cover with cold water; soak 20 to 30 minutes.

Prepare grill for direct cooking.

Remove corn from water; pat kernels dry with paper towels. Combine margarine, parsley, horseradish, paprika, pepper and salt in small bowl. Spread about half of margarine mixture evenly over kernels.

Bring husks back up each ear of corn; secure at top with wet string.

Place corn on grid. Grill, covered, over medium-high heat 15 to 20 minutes or until corn is hot and tender, turning every 5 minutes.

Transfer corn to serving plate. Remove front half of husks on each piece of corn; brush with remaining margarine mixture.

Makes 6 servings

Grilled Banana Squash with Rum & Brown Sugar

2 pounds banana squash or butternut squash
2 tablespoons dark rum or apple juice
2 tablespoons melted butter
2 tablespoons brown sugar

Cut squash into 4 pieces; discard seeds. Place squash in microwavable baking dish. Cover with vented plastic wrap. Microwave at HIGH 5 to 7 minutes, turning once. Discard plastic wrap; pierce flesh of squash with fork at 1-inch intervals. Place squash in foil pan. Combine rum and butter; brush over squash. Sprinkle with sugar. Grill squash on covered grill over medium KINGSFORD® Briquets 20 to 30 minutes until squash is tender.

Makes 4 servings

Zesty Corn-on-the-Cob

Mediterranean Grilled Vegetables

4 medium red or Yukon gold potatoes, cooked
3 tablespoons orange juice
2 tablespoons balsamic vinegar
1 clove garlic, minced
½ teaspoon salt
¼ teaspoon black pepper
⅓ cup plus 3 tablespoons olive oil, divided
8 thin slices (4×2 inches) prosciutto or ham (optional)
3 ounces soft goat cheese, cut into 8 pieces (optional)
8 asparagus spears
2 red or yellow bell peppers, cut in half, stemmed and seeded
2 zucchini, cut lengthwise into ¼-inch slices
2 Japanese eggplants, cut lengthwise into ¼-inch slices
1 fennel bulb, cut in half
8 large mushrooms
2 poblano or green bell peppers, cut in half, stemmed and seeded

Cut potatoes into thick slices. Combine juice, vinegar, garlic, salt and black pepper in small bowl; whisk in ⅓ cup oil. Set aside. Wrap each slice prosciutto around 1 piece cheese and 1 asparagus spear. Thread cheese bundles onto wooden skewers, piercing asparagus and securing cheese with wooden picks, if necessary. (Soak wooden skewers and picks in hot water 30 minutes to prevent burning.) Brush bundles with 3 tablespoons remaining oil.

Grill bell peppers, skin sides down, over medium KINGSFORD® Briquets 8 minutes until skins are charred. Place in large resealable plastic food storage bag; seal. Let stand 5 minutes; remove skin. Grill remaining vegetables on covered grill over medium briquets 2 to 5 minutes per side until tender. Grill cheese bundles over medium briquets until lightly browned. Arrange vegetables and cheese bundles in 13×9-inch glass dish; drizzle with dressing, turning to coat. Let stand 15 minutes. *Makes 6 to 8 servings*

Hot Off The Grill

For the best grilled vegetables parboil solid or starchy vegetables, such as carrots or potatoes, before using.

Mediterranean Grilled Vegetables

Portobello Mushrooms Sesame

4 large portobello mushrooms
2 tablespoons sweet rice wine
2 tablespoons reduced-
**   sodium soy sauce**
2 cloves garlic, minced
1 teaspoon dark sesame oil

1. Remove and discard stems from mushrooms; set caps aside. Combine remaining ingredients in small bowl.

2. Brush both sides of mushrooms with soy sauce mixture. Grill mushrooms top side up on covered grill over medium coals 3 to 4 minutes. Brush tops with soy sauce mixture and turn over; grill 2 minutes more or until mushrooms are lightly browned. Turn again and grill, basting frequently, 4 to 5 minutes or until tender when pressed with back of spatula. Remove mushrooms and cut diagonally into ½-inch-thick slices.   *Makes 4 servings*

Risotto with Grilled Vegetables

1 medium yellow onion, cut
**   into ½-inch slices**
1 zucchini, cut lengthwise into
**   halves**
**   Olive oil**
1 *each* small red and yellow
**   bell peppers**
1 tablespoon butter
1 cup arborio rice
3 to 3½ cups canned chicken
**   broth, divided**
½ cup dry sherry
⅔ cup freshly grated Parmesan
**   cheese**
**   Black pepper**
¼ cup toasted pine nuts
**   Chopped parsley**

Insert wooden picks into onion slices from edges to prevent separating into rings. (Soak wooden picks in hot water 15 minutes to prevent burning.) Brush onion and zucchini lightly with oil. Grill onion, zucchini and bell peppers on covered grill over medium KINGSFORD® Briquets 5 to 10 minutes for zucchini and 20 to 30 minutes for peppers and onion or until crisp-tender. Cut vegetables into chunks. Heat butter and 1 tablespoon oil in 3-quart saucepan over medium heat. Add rice; cook and stir 3 to 4 minutes or until opaque. Add ¼ cup broth and sherry; cook 3 to 5 minutes over medium-low heat until almost all liquid is absorbed, stirring constantly. Continue adding broth in about ¾-cup increments, cooking and stirring after each addition until broth is absorbed and rice is tender and creamy. Stir in Parmesan cheese with last addition of broth. Season to taste with black pepper; stir in pine nuts and grilled vegetables, reserving a few for garnish. Spoon risotto into serving dish; top with reserved vegetables and parsley.   *Makes 6 to 8 servings*

Portobello Mushrooms Sesame

Mesquite Summer Vegetable Medley

2 red potatoes, cut into thin
  wedges
2 medium carrots, diagonally
  sliced
3 zucchini, diagonally sliced
1 medium onion, cut into
  chunks
1 small head cauliflower,
  broken into flowerettes
1/2 cup **LAWRY'S®** Mesquite
  Marinade with Lime Juice
3/4 teaspoon **LAWRY'S®** Lemon
  Pepper
1/2 teaspoon **LAWRY'S®** Garlic
  Powder with Parsley
2 bacon slices, cooked and
  crumbled

In large bowl, combine all ingredients except bacon; mix well. Place vegetable mixture evenly on 4 (20×12-inch) pieces heavy-duty aluminum foil. Fold foil to enclose; seal tightly. Grill packets seam side up 20 to 30 minutes or until vegetables are tender. To serve, carefully remove vegetables—they will be very hot. Sprinkle with bacon. *Makes 4 servings*

Serving Suggestion: Serve with grilled meat, chicken or fish.

Grilled Greek Vegetables

1/4 cup olive oil
1 tablespoon lemon juice
2 teaspoons pressed garlic
1 teaspoon dried oregano
  leaves
1 pound assorted fresh
  vegetables, such as
  eggplant, summer squash,
  bell peppers, mushrooms
  and onions

Combine oil, lemon juice, garlic and oregano in large bowl. Slice eggplant into 1/2-inch-thick rounds.* Cut small squash lengthwise into halves; cut large squash into 1/2-inch-thick pieces. Cut bell peppers into large chunks. Cut onions into wedges or thick slices. Toss vegetables with oil mixture to coat. Place vegetables in single layer on grid; reserve remaining oil mixture. Grill on covered grill over medium KINGSFORD® Briquets 10 to 20 minutes or until tender, turning once and basting with remaining oil mixture.

Makes 4 servings

*If desired, eggplant slices can be salted on both sides and placed in single layer on paper towels. Let stand 30 minutes; blot dry with paper towels.

Mesquite Summer Vegetable Medley

Grilled Cajun Potato Wedges

3 large russet potatoes, washed and scrubbed (do not peel) (about 2¼ pounds)
¼ cup olive oil
2 cloves garlic, minced
1 teaspoon salt
1 teaspoon paprika
½ teaspoon dried thyme leaves
½ teaspoon dried oregano leaves
¼ teaspoon black pepper
⅛ to ¼ teaspoon ground red pepper
2 cups mesquite chips

1. Prepare barbecue grill for direct cooking. Preheat oven to 425°F.

2. Cut potatoes in half lengthwise; then cut each half lengthwise into 4 wedges. Place potatoes in large bowl. Add oil and garlic; toss to coat well.

3. Combine salt, paprika, thyme, oregano, black pepper and ground red pepper in small bowl. Sprinkle over potatoes; toss to coat well. Place potato wedges in single layer in shallow roasting pan. (Reserve remaining oil mixture left in large bowl.) Bake 20 minutes.

4. Meanwhile, cover mesquite chips with cold water; soak 20 minutes. Drain mesquite chips; sprinkle over coals. Place potato wedges on their sides on grid. Grill potato wedges, on covered grill, over medium coals 15 to 20 minutes or until potatoes are browned and fork-tender, brushing with reserved oil mixture halfway through grilling time and turning once with tongs.

Makes 4 to 6 servings

Grilled Corn Soup

4 ears Grilled Corn-on-the-Cob (recipe follows)
5 green onions
4 cups chicken broth, divided
Salt and black pepper

Cut kernels from cobs to make 2 to 2½ cups. Slice green onions, separating the white part from the green. Place corn, white part of onions and 2 cups chicken broth in blender or food processor; process until mixture is slightly lumpy. Place corn mixture in large saucepan; add remaining chicken broth. Simmer gently 15 minutes. Stir in sliced green onion tops; season to taste with salt and pepper.

Makes 4 to 6 servings

Grilled Corn-On-The-Cob: Turn back corn husks; do not remove. Remove silks with stiff brush; rinse corn under cold running water. Smooth husks back into position. Grill ears, on a covered grill, over medium-hot KINGSFORD® Briquets, about 25 minutes or until tender, turning corn often. Remove husks and serve.

Grilled Cajun Potato Wedges

Grilled Bok Choy Packets

12 fresh or dried shiitake mushrooms*
½ small onion, thinly sliced
1 head bok choy (1 pound), coarsely chopped
1 can (about 8¾ ounces) whole baby corn, drained and rinsed
1 large red bell pepper, cut into strips
2 tablespoons sweet cooking rice wine
2 tablespoons water
2 tablespoons reduced-sodium soy sauce
1½ teaspoons dark sesame oil
1 teaspoon minced fresh ginger
½ teaspoon salt

For dried mushrooms, place in small bowl; cover with warm water and soak 30 minutes to soften. Drain and squeeze dry.

1. Remove and discard mushroom stems; set aside. (Mushroom caps may be thinly sliced, if desired.)

2. Spray 6 (16-inch-long) sheets of foil with nonstick cooking spray. In center of each sheet, layer onion slices, bok choy, corn, bell pepper and mushrooms.

3. Combine rice wine, water, soy sauce, oil, ginger and salt in small bowl. Drizzle over vegetables in each packet.

4. Seal packets by bringing two long sides of foil together over vegetables; fold down in series of locked folds, allowing for heat circulation and expansion. Fold short ends up and over again. Press folds firmly to seal packets. Turn packets over several times to coat vegetables completely.

5. Grill packets on covered grill over medium to low coals about 10 minutes, turning every 2 to 3 minutes. (Vegetables will continue to cook once removed from heat.) To serve, carefully open one end of each packet and slide vegetables onto plates.

Makes 6 servings

Serving Suggestion: Serve with grilled shrimp.

Grilled Bok Choy Packets

South-of-the-Border Vegetable Kabobs

5 cloves garlic, peeled
½ cup A.I.® Bold & Spicy Steak Sauce
¼ cup PARKAY® 70% Vegetable Oil Spread, melted
1 tablespoon finely chopped cilantro
¾ teaspoon ground cumin
¼ teaspoon coarsely ground black pepper
⅛ teaspoon ground red pepper
3 ears corn, cut crosswise into 1½-inch thick slices and blanched
3 medium plum tomatoes, cut into ½-inch slices
1 small zucchini, cut lengthwise into thin slices
1 cup baby carrots, blanched

Mince 1 garlic clove; halve remaining garlic cloves and set aside. In small bowl, combine steak sauce, spread, cilantro, minced garlic, cumin and peppers; set aside.

Alternately thread vegetables and halved garlic cloves onto 6 (10-inch) metal skewers. Grill kabobs over medium heat for 7 to 9 minutes or until done, turning and basting often with steak sauce mixture. Remove from skewers; serve immediately.

Makes 6 servings

Hot Off The Grill

These full-flavored kabobs are a great side dish for entertaining. Prepare in advance, skewer and keep in the refrigerator until ready to grill. This frees you up for other last minute preparations.

South-of-the-Border Vegetable Kabobs

Spice it Up!

Texas Hot & Tangy BBQ Sauce (page 358)

Rosemary Garlic Rub (page 366)

Pineapple-Peach Salsa

2 cans (20 ounces each) pineapple tidbits in juice, drained
2 cans (15 ounces each) peach slices in juice, drained and chopped
1 can (15 ounces) black beans, rinsed and drained
¼ cup finely chopped red bell pepper
2 jalapeño peppers,* seeded and chopped
2 tablespoons chopped fresh cilantro
2 tablespoons lime juice
2 tablespoons red wine vinegar
½ teaspoon salt
¼ teaspoon ground red pepper
¼ teaspoon garlic powder

*Jalapeño peppers can sting and irritate the skin; wear rubber gloves when handling peppers and do not touch eyes.

1. Combine pineapple, peaches, beans, red bell pepper, jalapeño peppers, cilantro, lime juice, vinegar, salt, ground red pepper and garlic powder in large bowl; toss to coat.

2. Spoon into 4 labeled 1¾-cup containers. Store in containers in refrigerator up to 2 weeks.

Makes 4 (1¾-cup) containers

Tip: This tropical salsa bursting with fresh flavor is great served with chicken, fish or pork.

Texas Hot & Tangy BBQ Sauce

¼ cup vegetable oil
2 cups finely chopped onion
6 cloves garlic, minced
2 cups water
1 can (12 ounces) tomato paste
1 cup packed brown sugar
¾ cup apple cider vinegar
½ cup molasses
¼ cup Worcestershire sauce
2 tablespoons jalapeño pepper sauce
2 teaspoons chili powder
2 teaspoons ground cumin
½ teaspoon ground red pepper

1. Heat oil in large skillet over medium-high heat 1 minute. Add onion; cook and stir 8 to 10 minutes or until onion begins to brown. Add garlic; cook 2 minutes longer or until onion is golden. Add water, tomato paste, sugar, vinegar, molasses, Worcestershire sauce, jalapeño pepper sauce, chili powder, cumin and ground red pepper. Stir with wire whisk until well blended. Reduce heat to medium-low; simmer 15 minutes, stirring occasionally. Cover and remove from heat. Cool 30 minutes.

2. Spoon into 4 labeled 12-ounce containers. Store refrigerated up to 3 weeks. *Makes 5 to 5½ cups*

Helpful Hint: Take the chill out of winter with a summer-theme gift basket. Pack a picnic basket with a tablecloth, a festive jar filled with Texas Hot & Tangy BBQ Sauce, a loaf of crusty bread and a nice bottle of wine. A picnic by the fire is just the gift for the outdoors fanatic in your family.

Easy Honey Mustard Barbecue Sauce

1 bottle (10.5 ounces) PLOCHMAN'S® Mild Yellow Mustard (about 1 cup)
½ cup barbecue sauce
¼ cup honey
2 tablespoons finely minced onion

Mix all ingredients in medium bowl. Use as a condiment, or brush on chicken, pork chops or seafood. *Makes 2 cups*

Preparation Time: *5 minutes*

Texas Hot & Tangy BBQ Sauce

Gingered Apple-Cranberry Chutney

2 medium **Granny Smith apples, peeled and diced**
1 package (12 ounces) **fresh or thawed frozen cranberries**
1¼ cups **packed light brown sugar**
¾ cup **cranberry juice cocktail**
½ cup **golden raisins**
¼ cup **chopped crystallized ginger**
¼ cup **cider vinegar**
1 teaspoon **ground cinnamon**
⅛ teaspoon **ground allspice**

1. Combine apples, cranberries, sugar, cranberry juice cocktail, raisins, ginger, vinegar, cinnamon and allspice in heavy, medium saucepan. Bring to a boil over high heat. Reduce heat to medium. Simmer 20 to 25 minutes or until mixture is very thick, stirring occasionally with wooden spoon.

2. Remove saucepan from heat. Cool completely. Store in airtight container in refrigerator up to 2 weeks.   *Makes about 3 cups*

Spicy Peanut Sauce

⅔ cup **canned coconut milk**
4 tablespoons **sugar**
2 large **cloves garlic, minced**
1½ teaspoons **minced fresh ginger**
⅛ teaspoon **salt**
⅛ to ¼ teaspoon **cayenne pepper**
⅓ cup **chunky peanut butter***
3 tablespoons **lemon juice**

*If peanut butter contains sugar, decrease sugar to 3 tablespoons.

Combine coconut milk, sugar, garlic, ginger, salt and pepper in 2-quart saucepan; bring to a boil over high heat. Cook over medium heat 5 minutes, stirring occasionally. Stir in peanut butter and lemon juice; cook and stir 3 minutes. If sauce separates or is too thick, stir in 1 to 2 tablespoons boiling water.

Makes about ¾ cup

Favorite recipe from **The Kingsford Products Company**

Gingered Apple-Cranberry Chutney

Thai Marinade

½ cup **A.1.® Steak Sauce**
⅓ cup **peanut butter**
2 tablespoons **soy sauce**

In small nonmetal bowl, combine steak sauce, peanut butter and soy sauce. Use to marinate beef, poultry or pork for about 1 hour in the refrigerator.

Makes 1 cup

Corn & Bean Salsa

⅓ cup **olive oil**
3 tablespoons **FRANK'S® Original REDHOT® Cayenne Pepper Sauce**
3 tablespoons **red wine vinegar**
2 tablespoons **minced fresh cilantro leaves**
1 clove **garlic, minced**
½ teaspoon **chili powder**
¼ teaspoon **salt**
1 package (9 ounces) **frozen corn, thawed and drained**
1 can (16 ounces) **black beans, drained and rinsed**
1 large ripe **tomato, chopped**
2 **green onions, thinly sliced**

Whisk together oil, RedHot® sauce, vinegar, cilantro, garlic, chili powder and salt in large bowl until blended. Add corn, beans, tomato and onions; toss well to coat evenly. Cover and refrigerate 30 minutes before serving. Serve with grilled steak or hamburgers.

Makes 6 servings (about 4 cups salsa)

Prep Time: *15 minutes*
Chill Time: *30 minutes*

Hot Off The Grill

If using Thai Marinade also as a dipping sauce, place the marinade in a small saucepan and bring to a full boil. This precaution is necessary to prevent the cooked food from becoming contaminated with bacteria now present in the marinade from the raw food.

Thai Marinade

Carrot-Walnut Chutney

1 pound fresh carrots, peeled
and chopped into ½-inch
pieces
2 tablespoons vegetable oil
1½ cups chopped onions
¾ cup packed brown sugar
¼ cup apple cider vinegar
1 teaspoon ground allspice
1 teaspoon ground cumin
½ teaspoon black pepper
½ teaspoon ground cinnamon
¼ teaspoon salt
1 cup raisins
1½ cups chopped toasted
walnuts

1. Place carrots and ⅓ cup water in large saucepan; cover. Bring to a boil over high heat; reduce heat to low. Simmer 8 to 10 minutes or until tender; drain.

2. Heat oil in large skillet over medium-high heat 1 minute. Add onions; cook and stir 6 to 8 minutes or until golden brown. Stir in sugar, vinegar, allspice, cumin, pepper, cinnamon and salt; simmer 1 minute. Add raisins; simmer 3 minutes. Remove from heat; stir in carrots and walnuts. Spoon into 4 labeled 1-cup containers. Store refrigerated up to 4 weeks. *Makes 4 (1-cup) containers*

Balsamic-Mushroom Vinaigrette

5 tablespoons extra-virgin
olive oil, divided
¼ pound mushrooms, finely
chopped
¼ cup water
2 tablespoons balsamic
vinegar
1 teaspoon Dijon mustard
¼ teaspoon salt
3 tablespoons lemon juice

Heat 1 tablespoon oil in medium skillet over medium-high heat. Add mushrooms; cook and stir about 7 minutes until brown. Combine water, vinegar, mustard and salt in small bowl; add to mushrooms in skillet. Simmer until liquid is reduced by half. Remove from heat; whisk in lemon juice and remaining 4 tablespoons oil. Drizzle over grilled meats, poultry or fish. *Makes ¾ cup*

Favorite recipe from **The Kingsford Products Company**

Clockwise from top right: Carrot-Walnut Chutney and Chunky Fruit Chutney (page 366)

Rosemary Garlic Rub

**2 tablespoons chopped fresh
  rosemary**
**1½ teaspoons LAWRY'S®
  Seasoned Salt**
**1 teaspoon LAWRY'S® Garlic
  Pepper**
**½ teaspoon LAWRY'S® Garlic
  Powder with Parsley**
1 pound top sirloin steak
1 tablespoon olive oil

In small bowl, combine rosemary, Seasoned Salt, Garlic Pepper and Garlic Powder with Parsley; mix well. Brush both sides of steak with oil. Sprinkle with herb mixture, pressing onto steak. Grill or broil steak 15 to 20 minutes or until desired doneness, turning halfway through grilling time. *Makes 4 servings*

Serving Suggestion: Serve with oven-roasted or french-fried potatoes and honey-coated carrots.

Hint: This rub is also great on lamb or pork.

Chunky Fruit Chutney

**2 cans (15¼ ounces each)
  tropical fruit salad packed
  in light syrup and passion
  fruit juice**
**1 can (15 ounces) apricot
  halves in extra light syrup**
**1 cup chopped green bell
  pepper**
1 cup chopped red bell pepper
¼ cup packed brown sugar
1 teaspoon curry powder
1 teaspoon onion powder
½ teaspoon salt
½ teaspoon garlic powder
½ teaspoon ground ginger
½ teaspoon red pepper flakes
**½ teaspoon coarse ground
  black pepper**

1. Drain tropical fruit salad, reserving ½ cup liquid. Drain apricots; discard syrup. Chop fruit salad and apricots into ½-inch pieces.

2. Combine bell peppers, reserved ½ cup juice, sugar, curry powder, onion powder, salt, garlic powder, ginger, red pepper flakes and black pepper in large skillet. Bring to a boil over high heat. Reduce heat to medium-high; simmer 6 to 8 minutes or until most liquid is evaporated and bell peppers are tender. Remove from heat. Stir in chopped fruit.

3. Spoon into 4 labeled 1¼-cup containers. Store refrigerated up to 4 weeks. *Makes 4 (1¼-cup) containers*

Rosemary Garlic Rub

Rio Grande Salsa

1 tablespoon vegetable oil
1 onion, chopped
3 cloves garlic, minced
2 teaspoons ground cumin
1½ teaspoons chili powder
2 cans (14½ ounces each)
** diced tomatoes, drained**
1 canned chipotle chili pepper,
** seeded and finely diced**
1 teaspoon adobo sauce from
** canned chili pepper**
½ cup chopped fresh cilantro
¾ teaspoon sugar
½ teaspoon salt

1. Heat oil in medium saucepan over medium-high heat until hot. Add onion and garlic. Cook and stir 5 minutes or until onion is tender. Add cumin and chili powder; cook 30 seconds, stirring frequently. Add tomatoes, chili pepper and adobo sauce. Reduce heat to medium-low. Simmer 10 to 12 minutes or until salsa is thickened, stirring occasionally.

2. Remove saucepan from heat; stir in cilantro, sugar and salt. Cool completely. Store in airtight container in refrigerator up to 3 weeks.   *Makes about 3 cups*

Note: This salsa is very spicy. For a milder version, use only 1 teaspoon finely diced chipotle chili pepper.

Lemon Pepper & Thyme Rub

¼ cup minced fresh thyme
** leaves**
1 tablespoon LAWRY'S®
** Lemon Pepper**
2 teaspoons LAWRY'S®
** Seasoned Salt**
1 pound lamb chops
2 tablespoons olive oil

In small bowl, combine thyme, Lemon Pepper and Seasoned Salt; mix well. Brush both sides of chops with oil. Sprinkle with thyme mixture, pressing onto chops. Grill or broil chops 10 to 12 minutes or until desired doneness, turning halfway through grilling time.   *Makes 4 servings*

Serving Suggestion: Serve with garlic mashed potatoes and steamed asparagus.

Hint: Also excellent on beef, pork or chicken.

Rio Grande Salsa

Asian Spicy Sweet Mustard

**1 jar (16 ounces) spicy brown
  mustard
1 cup peanut butter
¾ cup hoisin sauce
½ cup packed brown sugar**

1. Combine mustard, peanut butter, hoisin sauce and sugar in medium bowl. Blend with wire whisk.

2. Spoon into 4 labeled 1-cup containers. Store refrigerated up to 4 weeks.

Makes 4 (1-cup) containers

Cracked Peppercorn Honey Mustard

**2½ cups Dijon mustard
1 jar (9½ ounces) extra-grainy
  Dijon mustard
¾ cup honey
2 tablespoons cracked black
  pepper
1 tablespoon dried tarragon
  leaves (optional)**

1. Combine Dijon mustard, grainy Dijon mustard, honey, pepper and tarragon in medium bowl. Blend with wire whisk.

2. Spoon into 4 labeled 1¼-cup containers. Store refrigerated up to 4 weeks.

Makes 4 (1¼-cup) containers

Hot Off The Grill

Mustards are a great way to add a mouthful of wonderful flavor to grilled meats. Use as a dipping sauce or as a spread for sandwiches.

Left to right: *Cracked Peppercorn Honey Mustard and Asian Spicy Sweet Mustard*

Mushroom Bacon Steak Sauce

**4 ounces bacon, cut into
    ¼-inch pieces
1 (10-ounce) package fresh
    mushrooms, sliced
2 tablespoons sherry cooking
    wine
¼ cup A.1.® Original or A.1.®
    Bold & Spicy Steak Sauce**

In large skillet, over medium-high heat, cook bacon until crisp. Using slotted spoon, remove bacon. Pour off all but 2 tablespoons drippings.

In same skillet, sauté mushrooms in reserved drippings 5 minutes or until tender. Using slotted spoon, remove mushrooms. Add sherry to skillet to deglaze pan. Stir in steak sauce, reserved mushrooms and bacon; heat through. Serve warm or at room temperature with cooked steak. Garnish as desired.

Makes 1½ cups

Citrus-Plum Barbecue Sauce

**2 containers (12 ounces each)
    orange juice concentrate
2 jars (12 ounces each) plum
    preserves
½ cup honey
½ cup tomato paste
¼ cup dry sherry
2 tablespoons minced ginger
2 tablespoons soy sauce
2 cloves garlic, minced
½ teaspoon salt
½ teaspoon black pepper**

1. Combine orange juice concentrate, plum preserves, honey, tomato paste, sherry, ginger, soy sauce, garlic, salt and pepper in large saucepan. Heat over medium-high heat until mixture begins to simmer. Reduce heat to medium-low; simmer 10 minutes. Cover and remove from heat. Cool 30 minutes.

2. Spoon into 4 labeled 12-ounce containers. Store refrigerated up to 3 weeks.

Makes 5½ to 6 cups

Mushroom Bacon Steak Sauce

Acknowledgments

The publisher would like to thank the companies and organizations listed for the use of their recipes and photographs in this publication.

A.1.® Steak Sauce

Birds Eye®

Bob Evans®

Butterball® Turkey Company

Del Monte Corporation

Dole Food Company, Inc.

Filippo Berio Olive Oil

GREY POUPON® Mustard

The HV Company

Kikkoman International Inc.

The Kingsford Products Company

Kraft Foods, Inc.

Land O' Lakes, Inc.

Lawry's® Foods, Inc.

McIlhenny Company (TABASCO® Pepper Sauce)

National Pork Producers Council

Plochman, Inc.

The Procter & Gamble Company

Reckitt & Colman Inc.

Index

METRIC CONVERSION CHART

VOLUME MEASUREMENTS (dry)

$1/8$ teaspoon = 0.5 mL
$1/4$ teaspoon = 1 mL
$1/2$ teaspoon = 2 mL
$3/4$ teaspoon = 4 mL
1 teaspoon = 5 mL
1 tablespoon = 15 mL
2 tablespoons = 30 mL
$1/4$ cup = 60 mL
$1/3$ cup = 75 mL
$1/2$ cup = 125 mL
$2/3$ cup = 150 mL
$3/4$ cup = 175 mL
1 cup = 250 mL
2 cups = 1 pint = 500 mL
3 cups = 750 mL
4 cups = 1 quart = 1 L

VOLUME MEASUREMENTS (fluid)

1 fluid ounce (2 tablespoons) = 30 mL
4 fluid ounces ($1/2$ cup) = 125 mL
8 fluid ounces (1 cup) = 250 mL
12 fluid ounces ($1 1/2$ cups) = 375 mL
16 fluid ounces (2 cups) = 500 mL

WEIGHTS (mass)

$1/2$ ounce = 15 g
1 ounce = 30 g
3 ounces = 90 g
4 ounces = 120 g
8 ounces = 225 g
10 ounces = 285 g
12 ounces = 360 g
16 ounces = 1 pound = 450 g

DIMENSIONS

$1/16$ inch = 2 mm
$1/8$ inch = 3 mm
$1/4$ inch = 6 mm
$1/2$ inch = 1.5 cm
$3/4$ inch = 2 cm
1 inch = 2.5 cm

OVEN TEMPERATURES

250°F = 120°C
275°F = 140°C
300°F = 150°C
325°F = 160°C
350°F = 180°C
375°F = 190°C
400°F = 200°C
425°F = 220°C
450°F = 230°C

BAKING PAN SIZES

Utensil	Size in Inches/Quarts	Metric Volume	Size in Centimeters
Baking or Cake Pan (square or rectangular)	8×8×2	2 L	20×20×5
	9×9×2	2.5 L	23×23×5
	12×8×2	3 L	30×20×5
	13×9×2	3.5 L	33×23×5
Loaf Pan	8×4×3	1.5 L	20×10×7
	9×5×3	2 L	23×13×7
Round Layer Cake Pan	8×1½	1.2 L	20×4
	9×1½	1.5 L	23×4
Pie Plate	8×1¼	750 mL	20×3
	9×1¼	1 L	23×3
Baking Dish or Casserole	1 quart	1 L	—
	1½ quart	1.5 L	—
	2 quart	2 L	—